Understanding The Rain

Understanding The Rain

*

Natural Lessons From An Oregon Life

Allen L. Scarbrough

Writers Club Press
San Jose New York Lincoln Shanghai

Understanding The Rain
Natural Lessons From An Oregon Life

Writers Club Press
an imprint of iUniverse, Inc.

For information address:
iUniverse, Inc.
5220 S. 16th St., Suite 200
Lincoln, NE 68512
www.iuniverse.com

Though essentially a work of non-fiction some of the dialogue has been altered for dramatic purposes. Some stories contain characters that may be partially fictional.

ISBN: 0-595-24310-X

Printed in the United States of America

Contents

1

The highest achievement of a human life is to alter the thoughts of men. All other endeavors are shortsighted, ill conceived and ill fated.

2

Not many men ever march to the shore alone, especially during a storm, or perhaps before the sun has wholly risen from its sleep, but I often do. One day I stopped at a beach near Coos Bay. I was traveling to Crescent City, a town I lived in for a short time prior to returning to Oregon. It was early evening. The sun sat suspended by the horizon as extended fingers of light, purple, crimson, and orange, stretched across the sky and back to the mountains. The fingers looked like a gigantic hand fleshed with light, clutching the earth in its orbit.

I parked and discovered myself alone. A towering embankment of sand veiled the beach, its humped shape pushed up by vicious winds along the shoreline. I strode to the crest of the sand drift and found the beach lying before me like a shield fashioned from coffee colored glass. There were no other men as far as I stretched my eyes to the north or the south so I plunked down by the water's edge and listened to the short, energetic waves thrashing against the sand. I watched as the sun sank until it kissed the lip of the sea. I allowed the wind to sift through my shirt and to caress my skin. I allowed sand fleas to hop on my leg. I discovered a stout log and sat back to gaze at the sunset. The shades of daylight deepened as the earth spun about. The pinks turned scarlet, the purples, black, and the oranges, chocolate.

As the day died, my thoughts churned as if made of vibrant water. I melted into the sea and sky and let my thoughts sip from the deep. As the sun vanished, the sky overflowed with tentacles of darkening energy. I shielded my eyes. I ceased to think. I vanished and received shelter in the echoes of the waves. Bordered by a billion points of light, I meditated only on the mystery before me. Four billion years the ocean had struggled, pounding the shore, hurling waves to kiss the sand. I felt like a pupil in a school that bestows not degrees, but serenity.

I unlocked my eyes and let a sliver of light trickle into my mind and I sensed an ache surging out of the sea. I remembered that the sea had witnessed a trillion days of solitude. Since the birth of time and space, the splendor of the universe had never been shared on earth until the coming of man. Man, a companion, an organizer of handsome things. I glanced to the sea and recognized a hunger thrusting it onward through the myriads of years. The hunger to be known, a hunger I shared. I understood this yearning as the call of a mother to her son.

I sat as darkness conquered the sky, as the ebony night, sprinkled with bulbs of starlight, lit my path back to the worried world. I yanked a quarter from my pocket and tossed it high into the salty air. I struggled to catch it as it plummeted under the drag of gravity. I walked and tossed as the glow from the stars shimmered beyond the shore. Then I tossed the coin too high and the coin struck a seagull in its side. The gull squawked and swung toward the sea. The bird elevated until it was shadowed in the brine beneath. I thought, how astronomical are the odds of striking a bird in flight? Then I thought again-not as astronomical as my being here at all.

3

Let me tell you what I learned sitting on the edge of a volcanic monolith at Harris Beach outside of Brookings. One summer day I drove from Smith River, California across the invisible border to a beach that lies north of the town of Brookings, Oregon. It is a remarkable beach, littered with odd shaped monoliths and protuberances that provide ledges and sacred places from which to inspect the world. I argue that from one summer day, and from one lofty place a man can learn what the world has to preach. But first he must decipher the language of nature.

I parked inside a straight, white lined stall next to a beast-sized vehicle. I rambled down a sloping path and passed players of games and fleshy revelers. Along Harris Beach's craggy shore stand the wonders of a previous age, monoliths that poke through layers of sand toward a sky they never attain. I crossed meandering brooks letting cold water run over my exposed toes. I listened to waves pound, gulls caw, wind snap, and fishing boats bellow. I spied a ledge along the shore and climbed until I reached the top where a level ledge beckoned me to sit.

It was a bristling day, long-lived, radiant, and bathed in heat that rose from the sea. Cross-legged, I stared out, absorbing the liquid universe to my front. The waves beat the shoreline, insistent, severe, bleaching the surf, agitating the uncomplaining creatures clinging to the edges of rocks. The round echoes from the waves formed songs, harmonies that blended with the sun.

I gazed at three fishing vessels put out to sea. I discerned fishermen as they dropped nets, and then hoisted them in a struggle to pull a living from the sea. How hard it must be, I thought, to work so doggedly. I looked around me, at birds, at crabs, mussels, and abundant fish, yet nothing struggled so hard to leach a living from the sea as these men did. Perhaps, I thought, man is struggling in the wrong direction. When a man is walking in the right direction, the universe provides all effects like fruit from a summer's tree. The fishermen toiled on, unconcerned.

In the surf I saw the relics of once-living creatures. Among the seaweed I discovered the body of a decaying gull and the carcass of a crab. Creatures that had stirred upon the earth, thirsting, hungering, reproducing, and were now fodder for the foam, destined to be preyed upon by creatures now deep in the throes of earthly struggle. I saw that one life scoops up nourishment from the plants, plants matured from the sun's energy, then that life is swallowed up, to the top of the food chain, until the sovereign is felled and his body becomes nourishment for lesser lives. How vast a circle the world is. A circle is the true path. Straight things are only the horizon's folly, fooling the eye into believing the world goes on forever, hiding the true line of the world which falls back to its beginning.

I gazed at two cumulus clouds standing guard across the measure of the sun, one to the left and one to the right of the imposing yellow eye. The sun rode through the pillars of the clouds in beaming splendor. The sky overflowed with the powdery blue of day. The sun, the eternal furnace, heated the air, which soaked up light, then fashioned the wind that howled inside the jagged rocks like a giant trumpet. And the wind in turn readied waves that pounded the volcanic rocks, striving to wear them away. The waves then made sand as the seasons turned, the sand then a home for new creatures. And the sand itself is made of mountains, mountains that crumbled through the pelting of rain and snow. The earth, subordinate to the sun, wears into roundness all that sticks into the air. Even the monoliths under my feet were wearing, grain-by-grain, to a smoothness mandated by time. Why, I asked, is everything striving to be round? The answer came to me on a wisp of salty air. Only men see the straight line, the flawless peak. As man watches his monuments of steel and glass mold themselves into circles, the universe mocks him. Wherever a man sets a course to, it will return him to where he began.

The ocean, chilly, vast, laid out like liquid cloth hiding the modesty of the earth. Where, I asked, did the ocean come from? The answer; the ocean came from space. Comets and ice balls tumbling through the deep collided over eons to form the vast oceans. Perhaps bringing with them life, or at least the foundation of life. However, the oceans are now more than a chemical concoction molded from the forces of chemistry. The oceans are now also a cradle from which all living sprang, a place that calls to me that I am born of water, and living by the grace of water. I am as man three-quarters water, a simple compound, yet this dual elixir houses most of the necessary ingredients for a human brain. Simplicity yields complexity when mixed together with time. Time is the key. Time stretches the fabric of space and collects the tools from which life is made. Man is made of water, soil, and time. We can see before us the soil, it does not speak, or reproduce or send pilots to the moon, and we can sit by water yet it never vibrates in the cavities of a man's mouth, nor does water ever leap to hold us in its arms. What then is left from which all the complexity of life is made, why it is time and no other? Time is the catalyst by which worlds spring into existence. Within the reach of a man's hands is the total mystery of the universe. It behooves men to heed the books printed upon the elements of the world. Only in reading these chiseled words will the answers to our history and our future be revealed.

My legs grew weary and twitched as the afternoon clawed the early evening. I quit the ledge and walked to my car. I'd spent a day at the Harvard of nature. My lessons well learned, I needed to sleep, to allow knowledge to penetrate my cerebral coil. I passed beach dwellers on my way out, men and women that had sat in the same class that day, and learned nothing they remember. So it is with men, some forge the future while others dither. But every so often a man comes into the world blest with vision, a man who can absorb the language of the world. It falls on his shoulders to etch the path, the way toward the peaceful circles. All of nature has been patient for our arrival that we might read the great books etched in rocks, mountains, valleys and seas. It is man's destiny to reach the stars, but only after he learns what it means to be alive, what it is that has made him. Our creator, dear souls, is named in a sacred word-time.

4

From where I lived my first thirty-five years I could peer west toward the utmost peak in the Coast Range Mountains. It is a shame that these frolicking, gregarious mountains were so ignobly named. I would have chosen perhaps, the Cloud Crest Mountains, for it is their duty to amass aggregates of clouds from the Pacific and to let them drop blanket-like over the Willamette Valley. The highest peak in this range is called Marys Peak. This name looks like it should contain an apostrophe, but it is correct as written. Marys Peak is less than half the height of Mount Hood, Oregon's highest peak. Yet it towers over its contiguous neighbors like a volcanic god and is the centerpiece of a westerly gaze from the grass fields below.

Along the highway to Waldport a turnoff signals the traveler to explore, it reads "Marys Peak Recreation Area." The road is nine miles long and leads to a parking lot that sits beneath the peak by about a half-mile. Along the paved stairway a viewpoint looks out to the Pacific, though it is rare that the ocean itself can be seen. Two meandering waterfalls also await thirsty travelers that stop for fresh runoff in the spring. Just before the summit a turnoff to a camping site sports bold, bright signs that my son placed there for his Eagle Scout project. As a concluding curve is breached, a large parking lot spreads out with a view of the Willamette Valley that is second to none.

One summer day, years ago, I drove to the parking lot on Marys Peak. When I arrived, late in the afternoon, there were three cars in the lot. I parked and stared at the valley. A tanned light haze enclosed the atmosphere. I made out the towns of Philomath, named for the conjunction of the words philosophy and mathematics, Corvallis, which means literally "heart of the valley" and Albany, named for the capital of New York for reasons that are vague. I saw extraordinary mountain peaks visible in the Cascades, due east. Mount Hood to the far left, Mount Jefferson, Mount Washington, Three Fingered Jack, and to the right, Three Sisters. The peaks appeared like stretched calliope notes bobbing up and down above the robust valley.

The valley stretched from the fields outside of Eugene to the fields that lay beyond Salem. Rows of grass and grain laid out in careful squares so that ownership could remain undisputed, but really, who owns a valley? It is too grandiose to be laid claim by the farmer. Across the fields I saw the residue of ten million years. Farmers had laid fertilizer to feed the inhabitants of the world. Yet mountains had bled into the land, washed by snow and time. Billions of creatures had lent their lifeless elements to form shafts of wheat and blades of grass. So man owns the right to till this soil, so what. The land is a finished good; man is but a consumer of the land. He owns the surface, not the substance.

Waves of heat rose from the valley floor and I watched the ripples leap to the edge of space. Heat is rained upon the earth, its energy a creation of the sun and is given without compensation to the people of earth. I watched as dust covered the air, stirred by farmers tilling the soil. The Willamette Valley is the grass seed capital of the world; most of the world's grass seeds are produced in the Oregon soil. It is rich, black earth, layers of silt slapped down by slithering rivers through the ages of time. If I were to ever farm it could only be at this place huddled in the shadow of living monuments.

I started to walk in the direction of the peak, a half-mile up a gravel road that allows government vehicles access to the weather station at the apex. After a twist in the road I stopped to remember a kiss from long ago. Many years before I'd sequestered a girl on a small plateau above the parking lot. We lay for hours, kissing, embracing and taking pleasure in the scenery. Though we both moved on with our lives, she-married with three children, I remembered that day as if it was happening again. As time passes, the heart savors memories when such things are no longer possible and glazes over the allure of our youth. I heard that she lost a child very young, how could we have foreseen such sorrow on that dazzling day when the world overflowed with possibility.

The altitude stretched my lungs and I lifted my head as I climbed to pick up the majesty about me. As I approached the peak, I stopped by the western side at an incredible sight I've seen but twice in thirty years. I saw the Pacific Ocean glistening in the distance beyond a small protuberance of hills. The sunlight reflected into the sky and I saw the ocean enclosed in marvelous waters. I didn't move for fear the world might cheat me out of this joyful illusion, but it was no illusion, yet it seemed no more a part of this world than the dreams of angels.

I jaunted to the peak and discovered a hefty concrete block once intended for a tower and I sat astride the block so I could see the ocean. Across my view a petite mountain rose up. It was roughly five hundred feet shorter than where I was positioned, but it sported a sea green meadow on its face that rolled down the side of Marys Peak and into its front like a lawn stretched before an ancient castle. Beyond this carpet of grass a plethora of lower hills struck up from the ground covered in firs and teeming with wildlife, such as deer and elk. The hills then gave out by the edge of the shadow of the sun and past that partition the waters of the Pacific pounded the shore and I imagined how beautiful it must be at that instant on the verdant sand, frolicking, drinking and devouring the daring light of the nearest star.

I stood and turned to face west, toward the Cascade Mountains and the fertile Willamette Valley. I watched plows stir thick dust and distant cars traverse the valley floor like an orderly army of ants. I jumped from the block and walked to the western side and flopped on an aged log that had been positioned for perfect peering at the world. Around me the meadow teemed with flowers, abundant, radiant, sheltering multitudes of bees. I smelled the bright breeze, filled with the essence of wildflowers and grass, seeds and heat. I wiped beads of sweat from my eyes and then looked straight into the sky above my head. The sky was as lucid as crystal that had been frozen in space. The air was bare blue and bright. I looked further and further into the blueness and stroked an item that belonged to the world, something I'd never named, a completeness at the edge of the atmosphere. I saw it, touched it, gathered it in. I knew this essence as indisputably as I knew the sun. It is a boundary that defines where the world may be. It is a carnal rope binding us to our place and forbidding us to be more than students of the sun. I reached up a hand in sober censure of this effulgent enclosure, but the casing of the world blistered me. Man is not to touch the abode of God, not in the flesh. Man is to learn the lessons of the joy to be found in nature. After this perhaps we will be released. There is no avenue of escape from this tethered time, except to learn what is before us and then to pray there is more.

I rose to leave and rocks skidded precariously under my feet as I angled toward the parking lot. I had a hunch that I'd come upon a forbidden barrier. I hopped into my car and drove the twisting road toward the highway, riding my heated brakes as if I expected them to stop the world. Even now, so many years after my experience, I still do not understand exactly what I encountered on Marys Peak, perhaps I will never know. Perhaps it was death itself, and if so I will one day make his acquaintance on more reasonable terms. I think he is a likeable fellow, all in all.

5

One autumn night I listened to the wind as it pushed through the trees in my yard. Leaves fluttered everywhere, landing on shrubs and patios. I bundled into a heavy winter coat and pulled a stocking cap over my ears and walked into the bleak gray night to watch the world dance below the moon. The sidewalks by my home were lined with elms and walnuts, their fruits fresh taken in to dry for Christmas baking. The leaves of myriad trees lay at my feet and blew across the road causing the night to come alive. I tightened my collar around my throat as the rain pelted my face and I tilted slightly toward the falling water to avoid the flushing of my eyes.

I watched the rain dive into puddles, splashing water onto my legs. I stopped and noticed raindrops as they fell past the streetlamp that penetrated the darkness of night like a miniature sun. I thought of days long past, days of youth when friends would play in yards, silly games that we invented. I thought of boys heaping huge piles of leaves and jumping into the pile with reckless abandon. I remembered a sad girl we never allowed to play. As I paced the bare sidewalk by the side of my street I stared into houses as I passed. I watched a woman washing dishes by her sink as her husband held her taut around the waist. I watched a cat stare out from a picture window and a tiny girl playing dolls in her room. I passed by an old, ramshackle house on the corner and watched an elderly lady, name unknown, sitting by a television watching Lawrence Welk, eating her TV dinner from a tray at her side. The vivid, silver light from her television bled out into the night and ran toward the moon. I saw, I listened and I walked.

The rain beat harder as I reached the end of my street and turned left onto a new street where bright houses were being built on a hillside to the north. I walked, now drenched on my legs, confident I was exploring a land as viable as the soil beneath my feet. I heard the droning of power lines and the distant whine of trucks sloshing through the highway that edges town. I watched a leaf fly down from the top of a great maple, twisting and plummeting to the earth; unaware of the great drama of life, death and rebirth in which it was partaking.   Autumn is a season of endings, of repentance, of thanksgiving for the gift of the fields. Autumn sings with wind and blesses with holy water from the sky. It is the season where leaves die and crops are harvested. The farmer pulls in his tools, his tractors, his plows, and waits for the deep winter that is only a forerunner to the birth of spring. Autumn is the season of death, but what is this death but a plowing of the fields to prepare for the spring planting. Nature is all a great dance, a round, a season, then a season, then a new year. There will be years as long as there are seasons and seasons as long as there are worlds, and when there are no new worlds in this universe, a new universe will be born. Life is just a season in an eternity of years.

I passed the new houses, some built, others crying to be finished and occupied with the clothes of families. I passed empty, finished homes that were ready for sale, and others with no roofs awaiting protection from winter rains. I passed houses with lush new lawns, fresh from the turf farm where they grow the grass straight and pure. I passed driveways and sidewalks where soon young children would play with balls, shooting, skipping, and running in an urge to grow. The lights from the streetlights grew dimmer near the far edge of the street as half built houses gave way to vacant lots.   At the end of the extended street, soon to be vibrant with the voices of life, the pavement inclined to a muddy slope that entered the hillside and disappeared into the dark fathoms of the night. Across the last spread of pavement a barrier stood, three steel rods placed in pillars of concrete. I gazed up to the top of the hill and saw nothing in the black except the tops of the tallest trees. I'd never been up that high before so I had no idea what lay beyond the scope of the barriers. My feet, already caked with wet mud, prodded me onward past the metal rods.

The rain abated as I entered the sanctuary of trees but the wind howled mercilessly. I was tempted to turn back. Instead I walked on sliding from time to time in the soupy froth. My legs were covered with mud up to my lower knee. I hiked warily into the cover of the firs and soon was taken from the realm of light altogether. The streetlights became a memory, the moon hid, and the light from the stars tucked under rain clouds. I could barely see the ends of my feet as I walked, but I climbed until I lost track of time and direction. I don't know what was prompting me up the hill, a stirring perhaps, or a simple need to explore. I had no clue.

I reached a little opening in the trees where a flat rock sat undisturbed. I climbed onto its abrasive surface and searched in every direction for a clue to my location. I found none. All light had been sapped from the night. I listened to the wind ruffling the limbs of stout trees. I listened as a living thing scurried through the brush to my right without disclosing its nature. My heart beat faster, my pulse quickened. I was lost not a mile from my home. This thought disturbed me. How so lost, so close to my own neighborhood? But I was lost. It occurred to me as I sat somewhat trembling that without light life is internal, dwelling within the passenger. I do not envy the blind man, though he hears the crickets playing in the grass. Man was meant for light.

Time marched on and the night grew brisk, bounded by omnipresent clouds. No stars, no moon, no streetlights, no notion as to how to proceed. I feared if I stayed I might develop frostbite, the temperature expected to drop into the upper twenties by morning. I was dazed, disturbed and full of the fear of bodily destruction. I knew my wife would be worried, as I never stayed on a walk for more than an hour or so. I began to weave tales in my mind of being discovered by hunters a year hence, decayed, decomposed, and bleached by the sun.

So I sat and tossed thoughts through the thick air until exhausted by the terribleness of the possibilities I took control and decided to venture into the black, busy night. I feared first for a falling tree, but then that fear gave way to the fear of falling down a ravine I couldn't see. I set out step-by-step, as cautious as a skeptical scientist. I proceeded in an unidentified direction. I stumbled on a tree stump and cut a long gash in my leg, which bathed my leg in hot liquid. As I walked the liquid quickly cooled and caked onto my skin. I started to shake ever so imperceptibly. Then the worst happened. I stepped into a pool of cold water, a pool of rainwater that had collected through the night. My unfit shoes allowed the water inside, through my thick socks and onto my skin. I listened to the squish squish as I walked.

Where I could, I gripped the small trunk of a young tree, letting it slide me down the hill. This worked until, unexpectedly, I would find myself rising again. My brain was overwhelmed by the sensory information, the sounds of wind and rain and fear. I became clouded. I'd never felt so alone with not even the company of a sympathetic moon. As I stepped up on a small mound a large fleshy animal bounded by. I supposed it was a grizzly, though such animals were unknown in the valley. My slight shaking gave way to intense quivering. I'd lost track of time, but guessed it might be approaching midnight. I'd been gone for four hours. Or maybe it was two or maybe it was eight, I didn't know.

I sat on the soggy soil and wept. I was a grown man but I'd never been so lost. The cold rifled through my coat and my soaking pants were more hindrance than help. If I'd only brought matches, I thought, I could light my clothes on fire and walk by the small incandescence they provided. But alas I'd brought little on this short walk. I thought of bats hiding in the trees waiting to swoop down and nest in my hair. I pulled my cap on tighter. I thought of hungry mountain lions looking for a quick snack and despite the fact that no mountain lion had been spotted in that tiny forest in fifty years, I feared the streak was about to end. If only I had some light, I thought, a tiny flicker of something. But there was nothing in my view save darkness.

I marched forward even though for all I knew I might be walking so deep into the forest as to never be found. I thought of my little neighborhood where moments ago I'd walked so gladly. I remembered my thoughts of children that I played with as a boy and of people tucked in their insulated homes, protected against the elements of rain and wind. I wondered to myself why I'd gone out on so blustery a night. I knew the answer, though it caught in my brain; I'd always been this way. That thought rattled over and over in my mind and wouldn't depart; I'd always been this way. I thought how we cannot escape our true natures and hide under layers of societal approval. The beast of our yearnings lives within. I ached to explore in the dark of night the stuff that is made of light. And now I was paying for my nature, just as all men will do. Our path in life is made crooked by the hardness of our hearts. Harmony comes only when the outer world is a true reflection of the inner world. Cooperation plus creativity equals peace. That is the grand equation of the world.

Then I thought an outlandish thought. A thought I'd never let enter my mind before. If I was a seeker after light in the dark, then I should be able to find the light even when it does not shine in my eyes. Nevertheless, despite this contradiction, I made a decision that changed not only the direction of my travels in these hills, but also the direction of my life. I stood straight and listened to the wind. It typically blew inland off the ocean from the southwest. I turned southwest and held out my hands like an eagle spread in flight. I reasoned that half a turn to my right would place my right hand to due north. I knew from observing the hills in the daylight that my house was north of the hills. I staked my life on this simple idea, though a change in wind during the preceding hours might mean death. I had no choice but to follow my instincts.

I turned and followed straight along the lines of my hands and if I thought I'd drifted off track I stood and spread my arms out again until my bearings were reassured. I walked up and down small mounds and then around trees and through open spaces filled with chunky mud. I was cold, shaking, yet determined. I'd found knowledge in the night though no light had guided me. I knew I'd stumbled on something profound, but unprocessed. Then I slipped on a rock that had been moistened with rain and slid down a gully about twenty feet. As I grabbed a shrub to stop my fall, a faint, mysterious light came over the edge of the ground as if a new star had been born that instant.

As my eyes focused I made out the plain outline of a streetlight in the distance. My heart leapt and my eyes watered. I steered straight for the light, unwavering. A few minutes later I discovered a gravel lane that I recognized as being a quarter mile from my house. I followed it to the edge of the pavement, turned left and walked up to my porch covered in mud. I could see the mantle clock through the picture window. It read four a.m. I'd been gone for eight hours. Gone on a search for light in the darkness. When I opened the door nothing stirred. I stripped off my clothes and threw them in the laundry room. I took a scorching shower in the downstairs stall, threw on a heavy blue robe and tip-toed up the stairs. I creaked open my bedroom door; my wife lay still, asleep. I slipped under the covers and was awakened a few hours later by the smell of hot bacon drifting through the room.

I stepped down the carpeted stairs and turned into the kitchen. My wife was hectic, cooking breakfast. She said, "You sure slept late."

"I didn't get back from my walk until four this morning," I responded. She laughed.

"Honey, I heard you come in about an hour after you left. I was upstairs reading in bed." I thought to convey the ordeal to her, but the thought of scaring her half to death stopped me.

"I know, just kidding." I sat at the table and saw my filthy clothes sitting in a basket in the laundry. I wondered what she had heard the night before. Perhaps she heard what she had always heard, the way it had always been. But what we think the world is and what it truly is are not the same. There is a mystery out beyond the bounds of time and space. My wife stepped into the laundry room in search of syrup for the pancakes and noticed the filthy clothes. "Dang it Allen, I keep telling you not to go out on rainy nights." Then she shrugged, "But you've always been that way." Yes, I thought, I've always been that way. But so has the world and all that is in it.

6

No man is peaceful who exits the world with his pockets full and his heart empty. I found this truth in the Mt. Jefferson Wilderness. Though the Bible says as much in many places, it is altogether different when the thought seeps through your own mind and into consciousness. The wilderness is an echo of how man used to live, away from cities, out in the shadows of mountains. So remote are the wilderness areas of Oregon that it is necessary to register your presence with the forest service before entering. I did so and was handed a slip of paper stamped five days. Five days marked the entirety of my stay, though in truth the journey has never ended.

I parked at the trailhead next to twelve or thirteen cars. My first thought was that the wilderness would be crowded, but I hadn't stopped to realize that those cars represented the entire population of an area of land more than a hundred miles square. Encounters with other hikers were to be as rare as encounters with bears. I retrieved my gear from the back, checked my pack, locked my car, and placed my new backpack over my shoulders and took my first steps into God's backyard. I walked up to a sign that marked the twenty-mile trail via grooves etched into a block of fir. The trail looked like a jaunt, a romp through level trails and around abundant lakes. Easy, I said to myself, for the last time.

I pierced the initial steps of the dirt trail and exited the parking lot. The proud firs soon encircled me and held me in the warmth of the sun. My head formed beads of sweat from the searing August heat and I wondered if I'd packed too many clothes. I traversed a small brook and scooped up a canteen of water. I bent down and cupped a minute amount of moisture into my dry mouth. The purity and temperature of the water startled me. The water tasted like the mountains and was as cold as any peak. It was the best water I've ever tasted and makes the bottled waters we buy seem tainted.

Spidery veins of sunlight bled through the canopy of trees as I hiked. Then, as if entering an unlocked cathedral, a meadow appeared and the sunlight burst out like a hollow wave. I draped my eyes. Across the green meadow wildlife flitted to and fro, insects cavorted and birds fluttered. The day was glorious. To be so free in nature, to be free of man and to be free of man's constructions, seemed to me like the gilded stairs to heaven. I was awash in sunlight, caressed by shadows, afraid only of the will of man. These were light steps.

About a mile later I encountered my first humans, clothed in hiking boots and khaki pants, burdened by heavy packs and heavier brows. I saluted, a simple rising of my left hand and they saluted back, though they did not move their lips to speak. They looked like ghosts out of a mist and disappeared on the trail like wisps of air. Towards noon, after a few miles of walking on level ground surrounded by water, trees and wildlife, I came to a large lake. To the side of the lake I crossed a low wooden bridge spanning a brook. I stood on the bridge and watched water pour down the hillside and into the lake. It was a cycle old as earth, a cycle that feeds the life that struggles upon it. We are not natural to the surface of the earth. The first living creatures on the land were as foreign as astronauts on the moon. But the earth is not the last vortex of life. First water, then earth, and then space. It is a circle as natural as the curve of the globe. We cannot stop the circle from closing. We are not in the last of our homes. The stars and planets sing to us. Just like the dry earth did so many millennia ago.

The trail wound in the region of the lake toward a red bluff in the distance. The waters were lucid and cool. About a dozen rafts floated on the surface, sporting a few fishing poles, but more dangling toes. These were slack waters that sleep in the shadows of the mountains to irrigate the woods. I discovered a robust log and sat and watched the rafters, day hikers only, there for the afternoon then to depart back to the world. They had not packs and tents, but food and boats and abundant drink. These were players, not students. Nature beckoned them as much as I, but they harkened only to the pleasure of the water, and that is all right in its season.

I'd many miles yet to travel so I hoofed along the trail deep into the forest. In three hours I passed only a diminutive accountant and his wife coming back from the furthest reaches of the trail. We had a brief chat. They had camped near a lake with an island a few miles ahead and recommended I stay there if possible. By the time I arrived in late afternoon my feet were weary red blobs and my shoulders raw from the heft of my pack. I'd only spoken ten words all day and that seemed a perfect economy to my soul. I unpacked the rudiments of trail life. My belly ached for the nourishment in my pack. I secured a thick, smooth camping spot near the water, possessing a clear view of the island, and I anchored my tent to unzip toward the water.

After pitching my tent I grabbed a black tarp and tossed it over the peak of the tent as insurance against the rain and to wedge in the heat. I fashioned an undersized lean-to on the south side with the overlap of tarp and placed my pack under it to be out of the morning dew and hide it from meandering animals in search of lunch. I unrolled my sleeping bag and made a pillow from my unused sweatshirt. Next I opened a bag of oatmeal and turned on my tiny propane stove and began to create oatmeal out of a small metal pot. The altitude made the effort a struggle. The thin air took so long to produce heat I nearly passed out from hunger.

I looked into the lake as I waited for the pot to boil. I scooped a small sample into my hands and detected myriads of life forms bustling in the water. I was perfectly aware that to get potable water from the lake I'd need to endure the painful process of watching water boil. The oatmeal began to flop about in the pot. I stirred it and mixed in a pinch of salt and sugar from packets I'd brought. I took out a blackened spoon and sitting down on the ground I ate with the ravenous zeal of a starving hyena. The meal quickly settled to the bottom of my empty pit and I took up the challenge of making coffee for my evening reward. I unsoiled the pot and began the process of boiling water once again. As I waited I discerned the red cliff to my back covered in fine dust and rocks. It possessed a sheer face and a sloping side that looked reachable in the early night. I decided, though exhausted, that I'd hike to the top and stare at the sunset. This turned out as both a stunning and stupid decision.

I sipped my coffee and observed the island for signs of life. None found. I did, however, spy a raft tied up to a tree fifty yards to the south. I dreamed up reasons to explore the next day rather than hike. I decided to stay and case the perimeter of the island, rather large by backpacking standards, and determine if I could avoid trouble. As the last drop of coffee plummeted to the floor of my stomach I warily placed my feet back into my hiking boots and started toward the bluff at the rear of my camp.

My feet stung as I walked, but not so much that they persuaded me to stop. However, the straightforward climb proved longer than I'd thought. Though the slope was simple the distance was not. But I'd come too far to turn around. I marched, hiked, cussed and sweat before reaching the summit an hour prior to sunset. When I reached the crest all my pain dissolved into euphoria. From that red bluff I could see for a hundred miles, or so it felt. I gazed into the plains of Bend and Redmond, into the face of Mount Jefferson, into the valleys beneath. I spotted my campsite with the help of my binoculars; from the peak it looked miles away. It might have been.

I discovered a level spot near the sheer edge of the cliff and plunked down to detach my boots. My socks were soaked in scarlet as blisters had formed, popped, and bled onto my bright white socks. I rubbed my feet and watched the ripples of heat rise up from the ground below. Soon the sun would plunge behind the mountains and a biting chill would descend on the wilderness. Heat was of the day; nights, even in the dead of August, were appallingly cold. I sipped fresh water from my canteen. It was sweet. I stripped down to my hiking shorts, which permitted the clean air to ventilate my perspiring arms. I was glad that

I'd made the climb, though my feet were raw. It was a meager price to pay.

The sun descended behind a barricade of sharp mountains in the west. The jagged blue of the day transformed to pale reds, dusty browns and deep, resilient indigos. The light had dematerialized from the backside of the wilderness as if tugged by the sun. I marked the trail with my eyes in order to make it back to camp as the daylight slacked, but in reality I'd have the moon, as it was to be full that night. As I sat I couldn't think of my life in the valley, my life of attaining goals and satisfying dreams. Out in the wilderness the struggle was just to live and grow. Men crave, strive, attain, conquer and dream. But they also, destroy, consume, devour, battle and kill. Men are two-edged beasts, only when their selfish side is restrained is progress made ready.

I glanced into the facade of Mount Jefferson, a peak over 10,000 feet high. I thought of the forces that shape mountains, the volcanic churning, and the tectonic plates that sink from subduction. At the peak of Mount Everest there are remnants of sea creatures. I thought how it is that men plot the future in neat lines drawn straight toward a goal of future desires, but we never reach this future. A twist, a turn of fate, an unexpected revolt, a terrible tragedy, tilt the world in a novel direction that forces a change in plans. The world was never planned to be what it is, it is what it became after billions of providential acci-dents. Yet there is an overpowering sense that the world is the product of infinite purpose.

The daylight faded and stars appeared, pursued by the rich, full light of the moon. I marveled at how man had reached the craggy surface of our celestial neighbor when computers had been so primitive. Man-kind struts his intelligence in fits and starts, failing more often than succeeding, but the grand lesson of failure is that it only takes a few paltry successes to fuel enormous progress. Life itself is the result of but a few great successes mixed among billions of failures. Ernest Heming-way once said words to the effect, "A man needs only to write one great book to be remembered, even if all of his other attempts are failures." This can be applied to all human endeavors.

I thought deeper into failure. When we examine the remnants of an ancient civilization we study its successes, the failures buried in their own time. Dreadful plays with atrocious plotting didn't survive Shakespeare's time and even Shakespeare's masterpieces only survived by a stroke of good fortune. George Washington lost more battles than he won, but his victories overshadowed his defeats. It is ultimate victory that is worthy of the fight. Failure teaches us more of truth than all the successes we achieve. We learn little from success, except that we have stumbled on a tiny piece of truth. But to succeed without failure is the emptiest of achievements. What is earned is learned.

The history of civilizations is the history of their brightest hours. Rome fell to the barbarians long before the Roman Empire collapsed, but Rome was recaptured and history records the event as an asterisk to Roman domination. Small victories are frivolous and short-lived; it is ultimate conquest that drives history onward. The dark ages lost much of the wisdom of the preceding centuries, yet today we have superceded all of the Greek's great achievements. To understand the future we must recognize the ultimate purpose of men. Temporary stays of execution will not prevent the eventual death of inferior ideas. Failure is the fuel of the future.

I stood as the daylight world retreated. New creatures, hidden by day, began to stir to hunt for food. It was as if the world were two places, a world of eyes and color, and a world of sound and shadow. I tugged my boots back on and winced in horrendous pain. My feet had swollen and scarcely fit my usually commodious shoes. I plunged along the slope of the bluff searching to find the last vestiges of the trail. I focused on the openings between shrubs and unearthed a path amid the darkness and the light. The moon showered light as the stars dotted the night sky. I could see only to walk and nothing else. I could not have discerned the silhouette of a predator if one had crossed my path.

I stopped halfway and gazed into the night sky. Out in the wilderness, absent from the city lights, the night was filled with a million dots of light, so plentiful as to give truth to the words "milky way', as if the universe had been switched on. I was filled with an odd conviction that life is in all places. That life has advanced from time immemorial and shall carry on to the end of time. Just what is the function of a globe if not to walk upon? Why should a sun blaze for ten billion years if not to warm the living? Why the anguish and indignities of man if not for a future we cannot conceive?

I followed the crude trail back to my camp. I detached my boots and stuck my tender feet into the cool water. A rush of pleasure washed over me. The pain evaporated, my thoughts diminished, and I sank into that bliss that is agony overcome. The moon reflected over the tranquil water and insects danced in multitudes upon the shiny surface. I turned an ear to the east and heard the din of two voices intruding from the opposite side of the lake. The voices chatted about the wonders seen that day. I began to do likewise. After my feet had absorbed all the liquid possible and the pain had numbed to a dull ache I ventured into my tent and zipped the cover closed. I lay on my sweatshirt in expectation of instant sleep. The voices, however, carried over the water and a discussion of wonders soon turned into verbal assault. Marriage, I thought.

7

I slept well, tossing and turning only on occasion. However, late in the night I'd heard the clop clop of gigantic hooves outside my tent. I'd been too warm in my bag to investigate. In the morning, when I popped outside, I spied hoof prints across the face of my tent, an elk perhaps, I thought, or a large deer. I looked at the black plastic pinned over the tent and realized it couldn't be seen at night by animals. I had doubtless escaped a good stepping on by the slimmest of margins. I positioned a bit of aluminum foil over the ridge of the tarp in hopes it might reflect moonlight in the direction of unsuspecting carrion. The sun bright and the sky clear, I began my second day in the wilderness. My feet were red, swollen and ached with a penetrating sharpness. The voices from the night before sustained their discussion in the early dew. The callous tones of the couple contrasted with the supple layers of warbling birds, humming insects and water plopping mammals.

I stepped to the lake to douse my face in cold water and shake the coils of fatigue that had wrapped about my body, but a small number of steps convinced me otherwise. The throbbing was replaced by pain of needle-like precision and I had to sit down. How, I thought, am I going to hike seven miles in these stumps? I rubbed them repeatedly hoping for relief, but only undulating waves of pain filtered up my spine. I hobbled to the edge of the lake and jammed my feet in the water letting chilly refreshment penetrate my aching appendages. The scheme afforded a trivial relief. As I sat with my feet dangling I again noticed the raft down shore and decided if I couldn't hike, I'd explore the island. This was a merry thought, a thought of childhood, a Huck Finn vision of unconquered domains. I lay back on the sandy shore and stared into the crisp, blue sky. I considered the thousand times I'd done this identical thing as a boy.

I dragged my carcass from the lake back to the propane stove. I rifled through my food pouch and located a small bag of freeze-dried bananas. I positioned one in my mouth and my digestive juices overflowed and oozed along my chin. I uncovered a measure of granola and mixed up a small portion of powered milk and fixed a grand breakfast. The granola, scarcely a favorite, nevertheless packed the raw emptiness of my stomach like a lump of coal in a Christmas stocking. I poured clear water from my canteen into my mouth as if filling a tank. I hoped to find another stream close at hand to replenish the canteen. The thought of drinking newly boiled water made me wince.

The intense chill of night vanished under the relentless pursuit of the sun. The cloudless day hovered overhead and provided a rich canopy for the adventurous day. I pulled on a fresh t-shirt, pulled on clean underwear and prepared myself for the task of setting sail to new worlds; however, the undeclared country lay in open view. I packed a lunch from my food pouch and looked up and down the hillside to my rear for running water. I observed an opening to the west that might be an outlet for fresh water. I wrapped my feet in two pairs of bulky socks and marched to the west. I climbed about ten feet up to the trail and walked straight ahead into the burgeoning sunlight. I placed a hand over my eyes to see the etched details of the trail. About two minutes later I encountered the married couple from the night before hiking swiftly along the hard-packed trail, their packs and gear stowed to military precision. I entered into my first significant conversation in two days. "Hello," the man offered, "You're not going to get too far with no shoes on." He chuckled as he turned toward his wife who had stopped to admire the island.

"I'm a little sore I'm afraid. I'm looking for fresh water then I'm headed out to the island for the day," I responded.

"That sounds lovely," the wife said.

"Well, we need to get moving. Need to cover ten miles today. To keep on schedule. There's a creek just up ahead," he stated matter-of-factly. A schedule seemed out of place in this well organized, yet unordered world. It seemed to me that the best application of time in the wilderness was to enjoy it for what it was and not twist it into something it was never meant to be.

"Good luck and enjoy the wilderness," I said to them both.

"Come on dear. Time's wasting," he said as his wife stared toward the island like a caged prisoner at the fields beyond his locked door. She sighed, shrugged and bowed back toward her husband.

"If we have to," she said, resigned to her fate.

"Two days left out here, have to see as much as possible," he said.

"It doesn't seem like we've really seen anything," she replied.

"Sure we have. We've seen the whole Jefferson Wilderness," he stated.

"Have we?" She asked. I bid ado and paced toward the outlet. I listened to the couple bicker until their voices faded into the vast organic expanse, absorbed forever by the lush green of the forest.

I came across the trickling stream and filled my canteen with cold, delicious water. I poured the liquid over my head until my hair was saturated then I wrung the tangles out with the fierce determination of my hands. I rubbed my face and neck and felt clean again. I found the raft tied up to a burly tree stump about thirty feet from the stream. I clipped my canteen back into its metal clasp and waded by the side of the lake until I reached the raft. The raft looked well used, doubtless built years earlier and used by untold hundreds over the summers. It was latched with sturdy rope and the large logs were just enough to sit on. I clamored aboard, unleashed the docking rope, and drifted casually on the still, translucent water.

I couldn't get the couple out of my brain as I drifted, the sharpness of their voices, the rush of their hike. It appeared like a recipe for disenchantment, as if their whole wilderness experience might one day be a blur without the aid of pictures snapped by an instant Polaroid. The couple's experience was like that of ill-informed men that meddle in the affairs of nature without concern for the consequences, and emotional meaning, of their actions. Life evolved in a fragile balance with all other life. Man hosts a myriad of parasites and hangers-on, all other mammals likewise. From simple structures to the complexities of human life the biology of earth has been an interwoven experience. Men are the apex of life, but are not differentiated from that life. We are not separate entities drifting on a sea of independence. Men are risen from the soup of molecules, bacteria, organic compounds and most of all water that inhabited this planet eons before the first man made fire. So to take this delicate balance, these interlocking circles, and to carve wedges of straight lines will cause disaster by and by. To walk opposite of the direction in which the world is turning will led us nowhere.

I've encountered so many men that aspire with their life but to achieve some conquest, to dissect the boundaries of the world and form countries, opinions, technologies and intensify production to satisfy the lust of an ever-aching society. Yes, man is destined to triumph in the company of stars and to breed into countless eternities, but we must not lose sight of the reality that we are not a being created to own the universe, but to sit at its head. So far men have succeeded only in being thrilled with their initial accomplishments. We have conquered disease (have we? They are reappearing in great haste) and we have reached the moon, but in all this achievement we have carved a hole where our humanity used to be. We are competing outside the realm of the natural world and if we persist nature will annihilate us. As we strive, the natural world will in due time retaliate. The great lesson is that man's goals are not mistaken if those goals are what I believe them to be. Meaning, world peace, an end to hunger, termination of life threatening disease, control of the elements, and education for all. If these are the goals of man (and I believe they are among the better elements) then it is simply our execution that must be tamed. Nature is screaming at us to take note, to pursue the example life has set before us like a Roman banquet. We can conquer the stars without destroying the earth. The redwood, though thunderously tall, never destroys the soil under its limbs. Cooperation is followed by prosperity; power is followed by destruction.

I collapsed on the raft and peered into the sky. I listened to the water as it lapped the edges of the vessel. I sensed a few flops of water that leaked into my shirt from gaps in the logs and rope. I listened and heard the magical voices of the trees. I listened and heard the thunderous roar of rough silence. I listened and heard the switch of the hunter and the hunted. I heard the concerto of nature in competing voices, and not in one voice hoisted above the others. I scooted to the fore to permit my feet to dangle and allow cold water to dash over my aching toes, to rush up my body and empty it of pain.

I placed my small lunch on my stomach to keep it dry, but the placing of food so near the organ of its decomposition just made me hungry. I sat up and scoured the shoreline of the island for a safe landing site. I discovered a large indentation between two inclined trees and rammed the craft hard into the shore. I lurched forward as the raft came to a halt and my lunch, so vigilantly guarded, tumbled forward into the damp sand. I jumped to retrieve it, but the raft pushed back as I moved and I tumbled into the shallow water soaking my clothes to the hilt. I dragged the raft to safety, picked up my dripping lunch and sat on the shore hoping the upcoming heat of the day might dry me out. But in the meantime it was cold, bitter enough to chill the marrow of bone.

The island, I could tell by the plethora of old fire pits, had been well explored. I suffered no illusions that I might discover something new on the peanut shaped dirt pile. The island was covered in clusters of small firs and provided scores of camping spots, which I dutifully explored. I used up the remainder of the morning circling the circumference of the self-contained world. There were no animals, save a few pesky birds, and the insects I encountered were less resilient than the bugs on the mainland. I considered going back and hauling my whole camp out to the island, but I changed plans when I realized if injured I might not be found for days, perhaps weeks. I'd encountered four people so far, but I'd been advised at the ranger station that there where only nineteen people camping past the initial lake. That left me vulnerable. I planned a hasty retreat at suppertime.

I salvaged a few bites from my soggy lunch and ate them uncomplainingly. I peeled off my shirt and pants and romped through the brush in underwear and a baseball cap as the heat of the sun baked my bare skin. If any one had seen me from shore I'm confident they would have thought me insane. Perhaps I was touched. After all, not many people venture into the wilderness then proceed to get still more isolated. But I had to admit it was invigorating to be this alone. No voices, no arguments, no decisions save the few needed for survival. I was liberated and in charge of my own world.

As I searched the perimeter of the island I drew closer to a small bay that had been used at various times as a camp spot. The fire pit was cavernous and well used. There were logs lain about to supply support. The grass had been matted to extinction and the branches of short trees had been slashed and finished into makeshift beds. I imagined myself a pioneer from the previous century and speculated how I might have rode out to Oregon from the civilized confines of St. Louis. I reasoned that I may have traveled alone, light and swift, but in retrospect I most likely would have turned into a fine scalp on an Indian's belt. Perhaps I would have deserved that fate. It seems the whites more or less determined to steal the land from the natives, using mechanical poverty as an excuse. But the truth remains that myriads of the natives were far wiser than the whites. We saw nothing of the dangers of overpopulation, overuse of land, depletion of resources, in fact we are only now, a hundred and fifty years afterward, coming to appreciate what the Indian's had recognized all along. If balance is a virtue then depletion is a sin.

Think for a moment about the plight of the natives. For as long as any oral tradition could be spoken there had only been identified to the native this new world and his nation back for a hundred generations. Any recollection of crossing the Bering Strait had been lost to their history. The native knew of no other world until the white man entered his domain in 1492. Imagine the stunned look on their faces to find out all they had known of the world was half mistaken. At first cooperation was attempted. The first settlers on this land survived only by the generosity of local natives who shared not only food but technology, the means to survive in the unknown land. But these two separate peoples, the native and the white had been separated by untold generations and the native had no acknowledged protection against diseases carried to the new world by the pilgrims. Small pox, among others, destroyed perhaps eighty million people. No wonder the natives believed their gods had turned against them. The white man flourished while the natives perished.

We pushed the natives back, back across the western frontier until a new excuse was set up to push them onto disagreeable lands in Oklahoma, South Dakota, Montana and Utah. Until the day appeared that we desired these lands as well. No excuse for our behavior was left unturned. The whites alleged they were entitled to the land because they possessed the technology to improve it. But in retrospect the whites also had the one object the natives lacked, the means to destroy it as well. Though our communal sins have now been swept under the carpet of rewritten history, the effects of our actions are still suffered to this day. We impoverished a people for no other reason than greed. This portends grave consequences in the future. Perhaps with the new casino capital the Indians will one day buy back the land? God may have willed this territory to the white settler, a case could be made, but in no way was there given a manifest destiny to pillage, plunder and exterminate. We thought that up all by ourselves.

The western United States is a much newer world. Old here means a hundred and fifty years, on the east coast there is two hundred added years of history. But in the west the wagon trains and the Indian massacres are still fresh. Out in Oregon and Washington few natives ever raised arms against us. Their greatest crimes were fishing salmon runs that we fancied for ourselves and populating choice coastal land that we sought for dairies and farms. Out in the west we recognize that our arrival destroyed a mode of life. We do not suffer similar illusions, as do our brethren in the east. We are quite convinced that we stole this country to satisfy our greed. By the time white settlers appeared in the west we knew our diseases killed, unmercifully, the native populations. We had already discerned that our arrival would mean death to thousands. We knew that we were little more than petty thieves. Out west we are honest in these things, but our legacy is one of guilt. In Oregon we have learned to love the land. That is the token of our guilt we concede to the native who has always looked condescendingly at our moral inferiority.

As the sun glistened in the lean air I placed my clothes onto my reddish body and sailed back to the mainland for supper. I'd accomplished no miles, no meaningful measure of the day. I could calculate no progress on a map, or even routes taken and explored. I'd spent a day less than three hundred yards from where it had begun, but in thought I had journeyed far. The visible residue of acts cannot gauge the distance men make in their lives. Some men die prosperous, but unfulfilled. Some men die poor, but rich in family. Some men die alone, but bursting with love. Some men die in agony, but full of peace. It is the spirit by which we must measure our journey. Our bodily deeds are little but obstinate catastrophes. However, after it is finished, our little life, we must be equipped to say-I intended no harm. A few simple words, yet less than one man in a thousand has earned the right to speak them.

I rafted ashore and bound the vessel to a tree. I replenished my canteen by the little brook and returned to camp. I was starving. I could do little but envision dancing potatoes and hamburger patties floating to the ground like black manna. Juices scurried under my tongue and I struggled for the patience to stay calm as I unwrapped a package of freeze-dried hamburger and potatoes. I stared at the unyielding flame of my propane stove and endeavored to will the water to a premature boil, but the water refused to oblige so I swigged from my canteen, but the water only encouraged an even deeper hunger, the kind of hunger that permeates the soul and demands to be filled by more than imaginary meat.

The sun sank into the tips of old growth trees and though hours before sunset the area glowed with a muted bath of golden light. I stirred the pot religiously and was rewarded with a rib sticking pot of pale goop. It tasted like potatoes rinsed in grease over-ladled with the leftovers from a butcher shop floor. I ate leisurely, then hurriedly. I swilled the goop down with a long draught of brook water and leaned against an old log in glorified satisfaction. As I stared toward the lake I saw the unmistakable figures of two women. Thin, waifish and encumbered with bags and burdens. I watched as they struggled to the edge of the lake. They looked immature, yet obstinate and unremitting. They prowled the bank for a campsite, but appeared to snag nothing but the sporadic low branch. I questioned if I should go and offer to help, but the ache of my feet and the heft of my belly prevented any acts of humanitarianism. I imagined they had begun the day in childlike pining for the wilderness and had by now realized there is a reason mankind suffered to build the civilized world.

I sat and watched, my eyes taking in their colossal undertaking. I felt bad, but they looked to be adults. I ought to leave them to themselves, I thought. Then one of the girls spied me out of the corner of her eye and tapped the other on the wing and I sensed four eyes bearing down on my body. My shame grew and my distance narrowed. It was as if I sat just a few feet away. They persisted in pulling on me with the power of their gaze. Little did they know how much I wished them to keep hiking in the opposite direction. Nevertheless, they started down the trail and I knew the trail led straight to my camp. I hastily put away food and supplies in case they asked for any. It was the strong sting of self-preservation.

I counted in half minutes until their arrival, certain they would cheat me out of every ounce of peace and quiet. Two women were about to stumble into my male domain and I'd be powerless to remain aloof. Moments later four feet stomped to the ledge over my camp and I awaited the inevitable question. "Hi," the tall brunette said, "Do you know of any good camp spots near the water, we're beat and need to set up before it gets dark?" I turned toward them and noticed they looked sweet faced and youthful. I couldn't help it; I invited them down by my log.

"To be honest this is the only spot with a wide enough beach to camp on. If you don't mind being back in the woods you can find several good spots."

"No, we really want to be near the water," the short blonde said. At this point my resistance to their company evaporated.

"Look, there's lots of space here. I'm by myself, why don't you join me for the night. I'm harmless."

"Yea, we know. If we didn't think so we wouldn't have stopped," the tall brunette said. They glanced at each other and rode up to my log and arranged their packs on the sand.

"Thanks, we were kind of uncertain what to do out here. We've never camped in the wilderness before."

"Could have fooled me," I said.

8

The girls, (I was too polite to ask, but determined they were about twenty), propped up their brand new tent in mere moments. Their tent, vivid orange, stood gawkily, a sharp contrast to my black plastic perfection. They situated their propane stove and started cooking a feast right out of "Julia Child's Cookbook." They searched packs for fresh vegetables, petite cubes of meat and potatoes vigilantly wrapped in foil. I was stunned into silence. As their water heated, the scent of fresh grub permeated the air making me slightly giddy. I had no choice but to beg. "Oh, that smells so wonderful, beats my freeze-dried packages." I reasoned that shameless flattery was the swiftest path to getting a generous helping. I also recognized that fresh food lasted less than a day in the summer heat and wondered if the girls knew that.

"Would you like some, when it's done?" The tall brunette asked. I struggled to think of a coy answer, so as not to appear too eager, but the aroma of fresh vegetables had turned me into a blubbering child.

"Y-yes, that would be a special treat. I haven't seen fresh vegetables in two days."

"We only brought fresh food for today. We knew it wouldn't last. Tomorrow its back to granola and freeze dry," the short blonde said.

"I would be grateful for any you might spare. By the way my name is Allen."

"Our pleasure. It's the least we could do after you let us camp here. I'm Cindy," the tall brunette stated, "My friend here is Julie."

"Welcome to my camp." I'd intended to speak to virtually no one for my five days, to seek and absorb the undercurrents in the wilderness, to grasp the vital harbors of the natural world, but these youthful girls possessed charm and I considered a one-day exemption. I thought I might be able to teach them, or they teach me. I welcomed their conversation and pulled out a diminutive bottle of Vodka, hoarded for a special occasion. The girls smiled.

We passed the small, helpless bottle of tonic quite a few times before the last drop was gently drained. The girls, I discovered, were undergraduates from the University of Oregon. They were looking to get in a little backpacking prior to fall classes. Neither of them had ever been to the Jefferson Wilderness. They lacked a confident sophistication about the wild. I quizzed them mercilessly. "So, how far are you girls planning on hiking each day?" I asked. They looked blankly at each other before Julie replied.

"We don't know. Hadn't thought that far ahead."

"Well if you don't plan it out you might find yourselves twenty miles deep in the woods on the day you're supposed to hike out."

"Yea, I see your point," Cindy stated. The girls giggling ceased and their minds twirled at the thinking they had failed to do. I thought I was making them feel stupid, but I wanted them to survive the wilderness so they might possibly help create a student group interested in preserving the natural resources of Oregon. The vodka took hold and I settled into the ground with the carelessness of a newborn. I looked up at the deepening sky and the treetops started to whirl. The alcohol on such a huge dose of clean air was overwhelming. I noticed the girls, too, looked fuzzy and tired.

"How far did you ladies hike today?" I asked.

"From the trailhead, like most people do."

"That's good, a good start. Do you like the wilderness so far?"

"I do. But I have to admit I didn't think there'd be so many bugs," Julie said. She pulled out a small bottle of repellant lotion and rubbed it all over her milky smooth skin. I noticed how it is that even in the wilderness the female form is delightfully round. Sandy asked if she could rub some on my skin. I obliged just to have the feel of another human being's hands on my recently untouched flesh. Cindy pulled up my sleeves and rubbed lotion on my neck and arms then she lifted the back of my shirt and rubbed there too. I didn't speak, I just closed my eyes and enjoyed the massage. Julie watched us, determining what effect two hands were having on my fragile male psyche. I reminded myself I wasn't in the woods to find girls, but to explore the outer world. They were causing me to drift away from the cause at hand, and I could have effortlessly given in to temptation. But I'd invested time and energy into my pursuit and determined that no matter how great a proposal was tendered I would decline. This righted my head and the trees stopped spinning.

"We would really like to get off the main trail and explore a little, but we're too afraid of getting lost. Have any suggestions," Julie said. I leaned against the log and let my mind roam, shaping just how mixed up with these two I wanted to get. I'd planned a side excursion to a little known lake three miles off the main trail. I'd learned of it from a friend. It was uninhabited and filled with solitude. I thought and then replied.

"I'll tell you a secret," I said as they gazed deeper into my eyes, "I was planning on hiking to a lake, about three miles off the trail tomorrow. It's uninhabited most of the year and I hear it's a great place. I'll offer to take you there if you promise to leave me the next day. After all I'm here to be alone." They looked at each other and both nodded enthusiastically.

"We'd love to," they said in unison. I liked these girls, they had spunk, but I wasn't sure what I had just gotten hooked into.

I shoveled the girl's delectable meal in ample bites. The smell alone, the whiffs of fresh garlic and pepper, made me salivate to the point of embarrassment. The girls ate in delicate bites, enjoying each nuance of flavor as I devoured. The girls cleaned up after supper and the three of us sat and watched tiny ripples on the water as the day bled into evening. I convinced myself these girls had arrived for a reason, a purposeful accident. Julie smiled and offered me a mint from her pack. I accepted and dropped the white-red confection into my mouth and tongued it as if it were a grand torte. Cindy stirred dirt clods with a stick and grew pensive. "Why do we humans seek nature? I mean really, what's the deal. It's comfortable back home. I have a soft bed, indoor plumbing, and fresh food. And yet here I am in the middle of summer out in the woods getting poked by mosquitoes and sleeping on hard ground eating dried food. Why, I ask you, why?" She asked.

I laughed. "Because you go to the University of Oregon, it's quite apparent you're not too bright."

"Ha, ha," Cindy said, "I suppose you went to Oregon State."

"Yes, as all philosophers do."

"Figures. So you're a philosopher then?" Julie asked.

"Not really, just a thinker. I hate real philosophy. Too boring. I like to read thinkers like Thoreau and Emerson. Maybe some Voltaire."

"Well we're English majors, so we've read some of that too," Julie said.

"English majors, out in the woods no less, that's interesting," I replied.

"Why should that surprise you? You have to experience the world before you can write about it."

"I suppose that's true. So that's you're ultimate goal then, to write?" I asked.

"It's Julie's ultimate goal, to be a writer. I want to edit, I like to mark papers," Cindy said.

"Indeed. You are the enemy then."

"What's that supposed to mean?" Cindy asked.

"I write too, but I don't like editors. They steal from the writer the clarity of what is said."

"Is that so. You don't think you might benefit from some editing?" Cindy asked.

"Nope. Only the natural editing that comes from living. Through living we come to edit out the unessential, the unimportant, the useless and the profane. What we are left is the distillation of our time. That tonic is what breathes life into our soul."

"Perhaps the truly gifted writers don't need me, but unfortunately most writers aren't all that gifted," Cindy said.

"I agree. There's a need for editors, but not in my world. I hope you get to do what makes you happy," I replied.

"Thanks. Hopefully we all will," Cindy said.

Julie interjected, "So what do you write? I write romance novels."

"Nothing so entertaining as romance novels. Who could compete with a good bodice ripper? I write books about my experiences in the outdoors and other travels, and I did write a novel."

"So you know what a bodice ripper is then?" July asked.

"That's where a man's desire for a woman is so enraged he simply has to tear away her underwear to get her. That I think is a singularly female perspective."

"Men don't lust like that?" July asked.

"Men love to tear off underwear, don't get me wrong. But it is the uncontrollable passion that is female. To act like that precludes a giving away of power and station, men aren't willingly going to do this. Besides most of the women in your BR's force the man to marry them before sex."

"Most of the time, not always," July responded.

"Then this is simply putting a plate of food before a ravenous dog. Once satisfied, the ravenous dog becomes quite tame."

"Exactly, I think that's the point," July stated.

"But then the man becomes the opposite of what stirred your passion," I replied.

"Humm, guess that's true, but the chase is what excites the female reader."

"I think its orgasm that excites your female readers," I said with a smile. They both laughed and Cindy mockingly beheaded me with her stick.

"They're fun to write. It's the same plot over and over but the details are constantly changing."

"I've never read one, but so I've heard. Any interest in writing more substantial fare?" I asked.

"Nope. I just want to write romances and have a family. Live a good life and enjoy my spin on earth," July stated.

"I salute you. Those are noble goals, if small in scope," I said.

"Julie always was a homebody at heart. I want to explore the world. Get out and meet new people, experience new countries and cultures. I can't wait to get out and live a little. School is so stultifying," Cindy blurted.

"Formal education is the study of dead knowledge. By the time it is written in a textbook it is only half true, by the time it's ten years old it's practically folklore. That's what struck me most about my college experience, that most of what I was learning was only conditionally true. Or rather true until proven false. The funny thing was how staunchly many of my professors defended their views, views they no longer hold. I've asked myself many times what the purpose of that four years was and I still don't know. I guess it did prepare me to deal with a bureaucratic world, but as far as preparing me to think it failed miserably. Most of what I read after college, on my own time, was more valuable," I said.

"I suppose we'll find that out soon enough for ourselves, but I agree with what you're saying. A lot of what we're forced to take is bullshit," Cindy replied.

"But I like your idea of traveling and exploring. Humans have no hope of peace until they learn that an opposite point of view is not a cause for extermination. Mix with the people of the world, find the common ground, and incorporate superior ideas into your own worldview. Dogma is a virus fed by the death of the heart. When we think and feel according to our own will, forsaking the dictates of the world then we come to see that most of what we've been taught in this life was for the sole purpose of keeping in place the powers of the moment, whether political or spiritual. Once a man has attained station in the world he defends that station with all the power of his body and mind. That is the cause of all war, and all ignorance, and poverty too. The idea that one man can elevate himself above another by his thoughts is the root of all human suffering. No man has ever taught so well that he could not also be taught. Even Buddha listened."

"Whew, that's a lot to take in all at once," Cindy stated, "I do a great deal of my own thinking. Don't think I'm some sort of automaton that does what she's told. But religion especially is hard for me for the very reason you stated. One minister gets it into his head to think the opposite on some issue from his church and decides to start a new church, which then splits off into new factions over time, and all this over interpretations of a two thousand year old book. I mean one church teaches that baptism must be by immersion, another that it's okay to sprinkle. One church teaches hell fire and damnation and another that all sins will ultimately be forgiven. How do you decide through all that what the truth is and how to live your life? It seems to me that it is the living of the religion that is most important not the doctrine it supports."

"Well said. You have just caused me to think about something I haven't really thought through before," I stated, " What you're saying is true. A religion is not a set of beliefs that must be followed, but a course of action through the myriad possibilities life presents. That should be obvious, but it isn't. A religion, in order to be vibrant, alive, purposeful, must allow the soul to journey through the obstacles of life with the most benefit and teach the cooperation of minds. The very fact that religions split over doctrine indicates that they are immersed in the control of thought rather than the exploration of the world. No wonder that church attendance is so low. People are not looking for a cookbook that gives a recipe for avoiding the pitfalls of life, which is how the Bible is taught. People are looking for a church that opens the avenues of the heart and mind, a feast of living so to speak, and allows the participants to eat of the bounty. Living water as the Bible itself would say. Where has this principle gone? No one is teaching the living vibrancy of the world. Every one seeks control, even the ministers of religion. But the more we seek control the more we lose control, the more we seek security the less we have. Life is a river, flowing, at times dangerous, at times placid, but always flowing. When we stop to take a look at a moment of life's existence it passes us into new forms. People must run with the river if they are ever to see the ocean. If you sit on the banks and cry 'come here and sit on this high ground and I will show you the way of the river', the river continues to flow and one day finds a new course that passes you by. But there you will still be sitting with your followers by the dry riverbed crying 'I will save you from the dangers of the water, keep you from drowning. Yes, but that isn't much of an accomplishment when the river can no longer be seen."

"Makes you want to start your own religion," July said, "Maybe I know just as much as anyone else about how to live."

"We are all teachers and students, always the two states are intertwined. If you break this bond you become neither," I stated, "I think you should start your own religion right here. The religion of Julie and Cindy. Take as your text the lessons of nature. Add the principle that all followers are also preachers, and all preachers followers and you have the start of a vibrant new church. Build no new buildings, take the water as your sanctuary, and let the mountains be your organ and sing only the praises of equality. Then prepare a table of learning and let your followers eat as they wish. Then let's see if mankind is improved or not."

"The Church Of Julie. I like it."

"But you are to be the only member," I added, "Each person must form his own church of himself. Then we are all equal. I began the Church Of Allen some time ago. I gave up on formal religion. I worship what I believe God to actually be."

"And what do you perceive God to actually be?" Cindy asked.

"God is the interchange of intelligence. In other words, God is the flow of the universe and not the universe itself. When we exchange ideas, share our thoughts and feelings, seek truth and understanding, we are experiencing God and are actually giving life to Him. God does not exist independently of the mind. We must call him into existence. You may say that God then is a construct of the human mind and that is false. God is called into existence by the seeking heart. He stays only if He is invited to stay. Only when God is extended to all minds will His existence be permanent. If we are not connected to the source of the water then we are not in the river." I noticed Cindy's eyes begin to droop and thought I'd blubbered on past her point of interest.

"That's the first interpretation of God I've actually understood," Cindy said, "I think I'll join the Church of Cindy."

"Great," I replied, "Tomorrow we begin to worship. Tonight we sleep."

"I love talking to you, but I have to admit I need some shut eye," Julie stated.

"Then to bed with us all," I said as if commanding an army. The sun had dropped over the horizon, but the sky was still filled with streaks of light. My body collapsed on the sleeping bag as I rolled out of my clothes for the night. I heard Julie and Cindy talking lower and lower then not at all. I passed into a dreamless sleep.

9

In the morning the sun was partially concealed by puffy clouds. It was the first hint of white in an otherwise seamless blue sky. It was my third day in the wilderness and I wondered if I'd been wise in asking the two girls to hike off trail with me. I liked them, but they were young and inexperienced. However, it was a moot point, the offer had been accepted. I climbed into fresh clothes and stretched my body high in the air, and then lowered it toward my toes. Dozens of joints popped as I bent. I stared at the girl's tent and heard nary a sound. I lit the propane burner and poured instant coffee into the pot to boil. The day appeared liquid with deep, musky air suspended overhead, signs of intense heat to come. It rarely climbed above eighty in the Jefferson Wilderness, but the day had the earmarks of a scorcher. I hoped to be up and moving before the full heat of the sun so I walked to the girl's tent and rustled the flap. Zilch. Not a peep. I pressed back the flap and peered inside. The tent was vacant. I heard rustling up on the trail and turned toward the swishing noises that I heard.

"So you're a peeping Tom then," Julie said as she appeared from behind a clump of stumpy brush.

"You girl's had me worried. I wanted to see if you were still alive," I answered.

"We are," Cindy replied, "We thought you were going to sleep all day. We've been up for two hours. We went to check out the red hill behind us. Have you been up there?"

"Oh yea, it's great. Look I want to get going soon. It's going to get extra hot. Make sure you have your canteens filled before we leave."

"Aye, aye sir," Cindy said holding her hand to her forehead in a mock salute. I slurped my warm coffee and watched the water of the lake ripple with an influx of debris from the forest air. Pieces of leaves, dried grass and the occasional water borne insect made tiny imperfections in the lens of the water. Cindy and Julie ate granola bars out of their packs then loaded their gear swiftly into marching specs. I rushed to keep up but only managed a chunk of an old Payday for breakfast. I knew the day would soon bring a gnawing hunger.

After we packed and readied, I smoothed the spaces where our tents had been pitched to enforce the facade of never having camped there. Julie and Cindy watched without questioning. Afterwards the mad trio of wilderness soldiers marched to the brook and filled five canteens to the hilt. We guzzled water by holding our mouths to the side and letting the chilly moisture wash over our tongues. I drank until a swishing noise escaped from my stomach. Julie and Cindy did likewise although with a daintiness that appeared ludicrous to me. The girls were charming and revitalizing with their youthful zeal, but they were young nevertheless and quietly amused me.

Julie guided us but had no inkling of where we were going. I commanded her left or right according to the directions charted on my map. The lake to which we were heading was unnamed. It would be impossible in the future to tell someone where it was I had camped. Unknown lake #345, I could hear myself saying to a future inquirer. Julie and Cindy, I realized, were cavorting with a man they had met less than a day ago toward an unknown lake three miles off trail. I could be taking them there to hack them to bits, or to rape them or God knew what else. I asked the obvious. "You know girls. You don't really know me. I could be an ax murderer. I could even be a rapist or a kidnapper. Aren't you being a little too trusting here? Then Cindy said the words that have burned in my soul for years every time I had half a notion I was a tough or intimidating figure, she turned to me and said, "You, no way you're a murderer. You have an innocent face."

"Thanks," I replied, " I feel so manly and mysterious now."

"You should take that as a compliment Allen. Safe men are hard to find," Julie added, "Besides you wouldn't have to rape us you know. We can be willing victims."

Peculiar thoughts crowded my brain at her words. One moment I felt innocent and non-threatening and the next like a man ready to break taboos. I walked ahead unable, or unwilling, to answer her.

We hiked in step along three miles of level terrain. The girls persistently adjusted their straps and played with their canteens, but I ignored them as I deliberated where to contact the off trail lake. I hiked as the girls hustled words out of their mouths as fast as they could form them. As I listened to their chatter I realized that most of it wasn't true, or at least was only partly true. These pretty girls had been raised in Oregon, gone to public schools and graduated with heads stuffed with mush and opinions shaped more by glamour magazines and television than by teachers. I was terrified at the depths they would take to defend illogical ideas. Our society is doing an astonishing job of brainwashing our youth, I thought, or is it just the advertisers?

We stopped near a plump boulder. I pulled out a compass and determined that the unknown lake lay over the ridge behind us. The girls peered over their shoulders at the forbidding terrain and winced. "That's how you get there?" Julie asked.

"Yes. We have to climb over a narrow group of ridges, then straight down into a canyon and then straight back up the next day," I answered. The girls stared at the ground then asked if I minded if they spoke privately. I knew what was coming. The girls huddled to the side as I sipped cool water from my canteen and contemplated the death march over the volcanic ridges.

"Allen, look we wanted to go off trail but this is insane. You could die out there and never be found. I think we're going to pass and hike on the main trail today," Cindy stated. I was beginning to have my doubts anyway at the wisdom of traipsing through the forest with two young girls in tow so I nodded my head.

"It' fine. Go ahead, perhaps I'll catch up to you before you leave." The girls smiled, relieved, and I kissed them both on the forehead and they waved as they fled into the undergrowth and vanished into the sunlight like starlight at dawn. They had slipped out of my life with the barest of connection. So it is with most men that we meet, they greet us as men and leave us as shadows, more real in our memories than they ever were in life. The ridges beckoned, my heart pumped, and my thoughts turned back to loneliness. I smiled, lesson learned.

10

I wiped profuse sweat from my brow, drawing in a deep breath as the light breeze fractured the near silence with the crisp movement of branches. I discovered an opening in the brush behind me and I opened the green door and entered. The first steps were easy. I pulled myself up the slope by yanking on branches and pulling on shrubs. After an hour my feet reached the sure hardness of bare rock and the rock bit into my soles like tiny spikes. The ridges, that had appeared smooth from the ground, now had the abrupt edges of rock sharpened by the elements to razor fineness. I wished that I were following the girls down the flat trail along the lake. But I had made the decision long before I'd entered the forest to find true solitude and explore it.

The ridge rose up along the edge of the basin and framed the lake in a natural bowl. Most of this volcanic wall had been hidden from the ground and had I seen it for what it truly was, a narrow, sharp, painful alley of uncertainty I would have searched for another outlet. But now as I walked gingerly on the sharp spines it occurred to me that the true struggle would be to get back up. As the ridge grew steeper I reached into my pack and pulled out a pair of soft leather gloves. I yanked them on and began stuttering on all fours in order not to risk sliding down the ridge to either side for roughly two hundred feet. I looked like a misshapen Cambrian beast.

The sun fused straight over my head for the sole purpose of inflicting physical pain. Being so high in altitude combined with standing precariously on a ledge, alone, bequeathed the sun a menacing face. Huge hawks flew overhead, off and on, and I kept mistaking them for buzzards. The trees, and the comfortable shade they afforded, had been left below. My pack grew heavier as I rose until it seemed to weigh more than I did. My feet, still tender, braved the sharp spines with ragged determination, but unable to glimpse my lower appendages I imagined them as shredded and red. After a colossal struggle I arrived at a flat spot on the first ridge and eagerly striped off my pack, dowsed my head with cold water, and stared ahead.

Across the end of the first ridge I spied two more ridges each requiring me to hike up and then down their spiny backs. Beyond the last ridge I spotted a basin that I guessed held the lake I was seeking. The basin appeared like a dark ring of death, devouring all living within its thorny reach. The black ring looked just like the pictures I'd seen of black holes as they consumed stars. I had no idea what lie below this black ring. I prayed it might be a lake with living creatures and not the entry point to oblivion. As I sat on the ledge I filled with loneliness more morose than any I'd ever experienced. This was not loneliness, I decided, but a kiss from the lips of death.

As a man seeks solitude and then achieves it, he finds his heart tugged in opposite directions. At once he hungers to consume the solitude and bathe in its soothing wake, at the same time he hears the company of men and his feet solicit to run to the voices that chime proverbial human chords. Men are both seekers and cowards. It has never been different on earth. The outcome of any exploration, whether for solitude or discovery, is determined only by a minute tipping of the scale in one direction or the other. As I sat on the ledge I let the two forces have play in my mind, to let them determine the outcome of my plight. With only a slight, aggravated sense of adventure I determined to plow on toward the lake, hidden from the maps and minds of other men. Fear of failure overcame fear of fracture.

The ridge began its bold descent just after the flatness of the ledge. My pack, once a burden, now became a blessing as it pushed me down the ridge. Gravity worked as I walked. No man truly understands what gravity is. It is still the highest mystery holding back man's desire for a unified understanding of the universe. Einstein said it was the curvature of space-time in the presence of matter, but quantum mechanics mandates that gravity must exchange particles. I myself believe gravity to be a shrinking of space and time. Nevertheless, I appreciated gravity's weighty presence after it had punished me all morning. I slid carefully down the ridge forbidding my eyes to focus on the depths to either side of the slim alley of rock.

I traversed the last spine of the first ridge only to spy the first spine of the next one. The sojourn to the lake was starting to take on the guilty glow of an ego fest. Did I really need to do this, I asked myself? What did I need to prove and to whom? I stopped and guzzled water before making the ascent. I needed a dose of courage. I summoned what little bravery I possessed and clamored up the ridge with the determination of a mating bull. I paced steadily, foot after foot, as I ascended once again to the heights of the wilderness. The second ridge, a tad wider and covered sporadically with small shrubs that danced in the breeze, proved to be an easier ride. I could lay the whole of my foot on the ground simultaneously and every few feet grab onto a spindly plant to pull me along. I started to enjoy the climb and as I reached higher along the ridge a magnificent view of the eastern mountains flooded my eyes. This shelve of peaks had been hidden from the first ledge and I hadn't anticipated any such sight. How magnificent it is to discover what has been there all along, but is revealed in all its splendor in an instant, like a dream that presents itself in one all embracing flicker.

I steadied my feet to handle the delicate balance of weight and pack so I might drink in a bit of the majesty of the view. I was the only conscious being within miles and I sensed an ownership of the view that made me rich though my wallet lay empty. It was as if the world had revealed a naked skin usually hidden under garments of cloth. The world became exposed, tender, elegant and alive. That moment I knew, as if the knowledge had been whispered to me from heaven, that the world has a soul. And if the world has a soul then so did I. I could not touch the peaks, but I nodded with a smile and I knew I'd been understood, just one insignificant soul speaking to another. Mutedly, I praised the earth for allowing me to reside on it and in return the world praised me for welcoming all that had been organized for man since the beginning of time. The world and I embraced and the wilderness, so untamed and raw, appeared to me more as an annexation of my mind than a vision of my eyes. I'd linked to the world in a ceremony witnessed only by the sun.

I rose to the tip of the second ridge and instead of a flat ledge I discovered only one partly extended spine. I wouldn't be able to stop and rest, I had to immediately start down the second ridge toward the third and final spine. The heat of the late afternoon bled me of moisture and I swilled water as if it were nectar. I'd drained one canteen and half of another. In two more hours I might cramp from dehydration or lack of salts. I needed to press on, to achieve my original goal, before the realities of solitude devoured me. I let the pack push me down the second ridge, which relieved the ache in my lower back. My feet marched with surety and I focused so intently on the narrow ridge that I failed to see a critter that flitted across my path. I reached the end of the second ridge and paused in the tiny indentation before ascending the last backbone of hardened lava.

I watched as waves of intense heat fluttered in the hot August air. I wiped the fluids from my upper body and thanked God I'd come this way alone. I did not miss the girls at all. It had been foolish to invite them and fate had intervened and spared me the misery of company. Though I had not spoken a word in hours I'd carried on a conversation with the land and the sky. My tongue was exhausted from the words that had never left my mouth. Off in the distance I could just make out the lip of the black ring. It was darker and more menacing the closer I came. It was as if the black ring was a sign that warned the weak not to enter, or a sign that paved the pathway for the determined. I wasn't sure which category I fell into.

I stepped forward and ascended toward the final ridge. The edges of my feet latched onto the sharper spines of the new ridge and confidence flew into me as I lifted toward the blue-white sky. My day was approaching magnificence. I'd let the world enter me in a new manner, had let the sky breath for me, and had let the wind and heat drag me. I was alive, not the half-shelled life of the valley, or of civilization, but the bursting, sober, hungering living that only the beholders of silence know. My legs filled with energy, my arms bustled with electric twitching, my eyes honed and my heart pumped blood at galling levels. All my thoughts were of the next step, the next breath, the next minute and the next life. I bathed in the tub of the divine and stepped unsoiled, unembellished, naked, and blossoming en route to the next revelation hiding just over the last of three ridges.

As the sun beat on my head the last ridge proved a tough foe. The ridge narrowed to a sliver and the spines grew sharp and jagged. I was close to exhaustion. The hours of careful climbing had sapped my strength, depleted my reserves. I was a feeble man on a solid foundation praying not to plunge to either side. I clamped on my wandering thoughts and forced them into a tight bundle. I climbed one point at a time and listened only to the beat of my heart and saw only the dreary landscape three feet in front of my eyes. The day passed into late afternoon as the heat reflected off the rocks. I swilled the last of my water as I stood up on a wide spine and stared into the sky.

The black hole had grown larger with the passage of time but it had softened its harsh appearance. I could see into the basin below the ring and thought I could see the faint outline of a lake. My spirits revived at the thought of a few moments sitting with my feet dangling in the cold water and I chastened myself for the final assault. I reached the highest point on ridge three a half hour later and I stood at the apex and peered into the basin beneath. I could see the outer shell of a lake. The far edge reflected sunlight toward my eyes with bold reassurance. I looked across the black rim to plot my path down into the basin and discovered a soft slope on the northern edge that looked to lead down in a methodical, yet meandering way. The travail and pain of the last few hours seemed miniscule in the moment of fresh inspiration that flooded me. The journey will be worth it, I said to no one.

I ambled down the backside of the last ridge and commenced a soft descent on pulverized volcanic rock that possessed the feel and shape of fine gravel. My only complaint was that the black rock was hot; my feet felt like stumps as I walked the slow decline toward the lost lake without a name. I decided to name the lake 'Three Ridge Lake" in honor of the three hellish backbones I traversed just to enjoy the lake's blue bounty. As I walked the sloping path of volcanic material, the lake came into full view and the sum of it blew away my preconceptions of how striking a natural object could be. It was the most stunning lake and shore I'd ever seen. And best of all, I was the only breathing soul within three miles of it. I smiled at the realization that the lake, the shore, the sky and the creatures of the basin were all mine to enjoy as if it were my private domain.

The gentle slope of the black path was heavenly compared to the horrific steps of the ridges. I held no doubt as to why this lake wasn't on the map. Only the insane would ever venture this far into the unknown. No normal person would ever venture to see the sight that lay before my eyes. Perhaps normal isn't all its cracked up to be if it denies the soul these gorgeous temples. I slapped one happy foot in front of the other and by suppertime I'd reached the edge of the lake. I found an opening near the water and laid my pack on the ground letting out a huge grunt that could have been heard across the lake if there had been ears to receive it. A few birds flew overhead and insects abounded, but little else shared the lake with me. I was alone, but I was devoid of loneliness.

The water in the lake was clear blue. That meant little or no algae. I could have drunk straight from the water but thought I should not risk dysentery so far away from civilization. So I would boil. I scouted the small edge of the water. I decided that no large mammals lived nearby and proceeded to pitch my tent in the flat opening near the water. The flat area was covered in fine volcanic rock, just like the path, and I hoped the black powder might provide a fantastic natural mattress. I sheltered my tent with the same black plastic as before and now it became invisible. Only the whiteness of my face stood out from the black shoreline as if a bodiless ghost had invaded sacred grounds. I held my hands up to my mouth and bellowed across the water, "I am a ghost. I'm not real." Twelve echoes ran back, overlapping one another until the sharp sounds died in the bowels of the lake. I was an intruder and had committed a sin by my disturbance. I sealed my mouth shut.

I swiftly set up my propane stove. I was hungry beyond ravenous. Just the smell of freeze dried meat sent undulating waves of saliva over my tongue. I boiled water first and placed it in an extra pan to cool. Then I sank the dried packaged product into a new batch of water and waited eagerly for it to boil. I was higher up than the previous day so boiling took even longer. I could do nothing but stare at the pot nervously awaiting the first bubble of heat. I searched for a log to lie against, but found only a modest limb that had drifted along the lake for numberless years before settling in a spot just to my left. I placed it near the stove and leaned back on the log, though it made me virtually horizontal to do so.

The water formed its first bubble after many minutes and I couldn't restrain myself from scooping half heated meat out of the pan with my bare hands. I gritted my teeth and ate some of the meat even though it was still cool and unpleasant. I fished my utensil set out of my pack along with a small folding plate and spooned out the brownish goop with my trembling hand as guide. A little of the goop spilled onto the ground and I mentally cursed. I lay back on the log and spooned large heaps of the foodstuff into my wet mouth. It tasted rich; bursting with flavor and my mouth achieved a half orgasm as it pulverized the pulp into digestible shape. I cried three gigantic tears just at the thought of so heavenly a meal. I had no idea freeze-dried meat pulp could taste better than New York Steak.

I finished the meal quickly and sifted through the depths of my pack and found a fruit roll that I used for desert. The sugary sweetness brought strength back into my limbs and I cleaned up the pots and finished making my bed for the night. The sun fell behind the black hole and I lit the propane stove again to achieve a sense of light. I sat staring out toward the lake. The surface was smoother than the first lake beside the popular trail. A few insects began their nightly dance atop the water, but the rest of the shore was as undisturbed as a lifeless earth. There were several short trees near the edge of the lake and some shrubbery, but much of the shore was black volcanic residue laid down in the last great cataclysm thousands of years before the arrival of man. The Cascade Mountains are old in relation to man, but young compared to the last four billion years.

My thoughts pulled toward time. So much history lay before my eyes I couldn't ignore it. I thought of the meaning of my few years when I lived in a universe that had already existed for fourteen billion years and is destined to emit starlight for another hundred trillion years. Though we have evolved and are at present basking in the light of a middle-aged sun we are at this time, alive, breathing, and exploring in the early years of the universe. We are children of the dawn, of the eternal morning, and are destined to paint a path to the stars. More will come after us than has preceded us. We are a part of the great history to one-day be written by an extra advanced civilization. They will discover our history in the radio and television waves we have broadcast. The earth itself, however, will be little more than cinder in that far future age.

As the night covered the basin, shaped by the lake, a shaft of stars filled the dark blue of evening. I'd seen stars, myriads, but in that reverberating air I discovered the whole of existence back to the dawn of starlight, back to the opaque barrier standing within 300,000 light years from the big bang, or so it seemed. For to me, there were too many vivid, effulgent lights to number by any other process than to take in the whole of the history of space. I was stuffed with stars, nothing but stars. Stars danced across the still water, stars ate of the dark of night, and stars filled my expanding head boring deep into my memories. Stars crossed the ocean of space, pirouetted across the disk of distant galaxies, and stars shone through the eternal mystery and illuminated my eyes. I existed as starlight and was made of starlight. I dreamed in starlight and bathed in starlight. I reproduced in starlight. I sang by the starlight. All was starlight, all was found in the soft glow of suns formed billions of years ago in a vast void of gas and dust, pressure then condensing the gas and dust, and then the remnants of these stars supplying the heavy elements for our sun's creation. I discovered in the light of these stars the eyes of God. For knowledge of God must also come to earth by starlight. Starlight is the only path from world to world. And even starlight is woefully inadequate to the task. Our neighbors in the night are as mysterious to us now as they will ever be in the future. Starlight travels unimaginably fast, but the universe is bigger than the unimaginable.

I opened my ears and listened to the warbles of the living lake. I heard two fish vault to the surface to catch bugs. I heard mysterious buzzing, mosquitoes, and raced to my pack to bombard my face ands arms with repellant. I smelled of chemicals, tart and bitter. The little pests swam above my head, but dared not land. I heard the soft swishing of miniscule waves. The stillness deepened and I heard the air folding into layers of returning heat and icicle cold. I strapped on my thick sweatshirt and bundled myself, embracing the tiny fire from my stove as if it was the last light of the world. I heard the echoes from the earth rebounding out to the deafness of space. Night blossomed and I lay like an insect on the surface of the rounded dust. Then I heard a voice.

11

"Hey there, partner," a large full-bodied voice echoed across the stillness. I clutched my lock blade knife to my side and searched the horizon for the source of the mysterious voice. I spied a rotunderous lump of humanity about sixty paces to the south and could just make out the silver hair of an old man as the starlight shimmered across its greasy whiteness.

"Hello there. Are you friendly?" I questioned.

"As far as I know. I'm as lost as I can be. Any clue as to where we are?"

"Come over by the light and I'll show you on the map," I offered.

"All righty, be right there." The blob marched straight toward the light. With the body's gigantic pack making an outline befitting a giant, I closed my fingers around my knife. The body appeared out of the dank shadows into my stove's light. A kindly, gentlemanly old man appeared in the glow and all fear escaped me.

"How in the hell did you find this place without knowing where it was. This isn't even a named lake?"

"Don't know partner. I was walking on a trail and the next thing I knew I was headed toward this lake. Took a wrong turn somewhere I reckon."

"Yea, I reckon. You hiked much in the past?"

"Yep, a lot, but never up here. My god there's three hundred miles of trails up here."

"Yea I know that's why you need a map."

"Guess so, but I never put much store in them things. I always figured I could find my way by the stars."

"Well, my friend, out here the stars point to everywhere and nowhere."

"I found that out, the hard way. Say, you mind if I borrow a little of that heat to cook some dinner. I could eat a pile of cardboard about now."

"Sure, knock yourself out." The silvery man slipped off his pack and pulled out a package of freeze-dried soup. I poured the contents of my biggest canteen into my pot and slipped it on the stove as the man dunked his crusty packet into the cold water. He smiled at my assistance. This gentle old man carried nothing of hatred or fear of man. He was as simple as men can be, and as soothing as a rainbow at the end of a ceaseless rain.

"My name's Allen by the way. I've been out here for three days. I'll be hiking out day after tomorrow. How about yourself?"

"Well, my name's Jack. I've been out in the wilderness since the seventeenth of June, save for a few hike outs for groceries. I'll be out here one more week then it's back to Montana to teach school in the fall."

"School teacher then. What grade?"

"Middle school mostly. I teach wood shop. I like the kids before they develop all that attitude. But I spend summers out in the woods. I go from trailhead to trailhead trying to get away from it all. I've been all over the United States."

"How long have you been doing this? Hiking I mean."

"I started about ten years ago after my wife died of Leukemia."

"Sorry to hear it."

"She was a wonderful woman. I'll never find another like her." Just then his water came to a full boil and he switched his attention to his supper. I'd struck a nerve and discovered Jack was a man who had loved deeply and well.

"You never know, surprises sometimes leap out of nowhere." Jack stared into the pot, sighed, and nodded his head. I sat cross-legged as Jack stirred the pot with the vigor of a young man. His old body appeared taught and toned, chiseled by time and trouble. Jack was thirty years my senior, but in wisdom I felt the gap was more like a hundred years. I'd never encountered the harsh events that Jack knew like family.

"Pardon me for eating in front of ya. I assume you've already eaten or I'd offer some to ya."

"That's okay Jack. I'm stuffed. It's all yours."

Jack plopped onto his haunches and ladled the slop into his mouth with the indelicacy of a starving Biafran. Three minutes later he laid the pot on the ground and wiped his mouth with the sleeve of his t-shirt. "Thanks, partner. I appreciate the heat. I guess I should be setting up shop for the night. Need to find my way out of here in the morning."

"Be my guest. You can pitch your tent right here. Can't sleep out because of the mosquitoes."

"Yea, I noticed. I practically had to dump a bottle of repellent on my skin just after sundown."

"How did you find your way in the dark. The ground's so black here?"

"Didn't, I've been sitting over on the other side of the lake since sundown. I finally noticed your fire and decided to come by and see if you knew where we were at."

"I know where we're at, but it's not easy getting to or getting out of."

"What do you mean? It's practically flat."

"I had to climb over three narrow-spined ridges to get here. One false step and boom."

"You musta come a different way. This lake is a flat walk from the back of a meadow to the other side of the main trail, I just got lost and thought the lake was my best chance for finding somebody. I want to head west and just wanted to know if there was an easy way out. Guess you've answered that question for me" I grabbed my map and thrust it near the fire still emanating from the stove. I glanced over and over at the trail and sure enough I'd made a terrible blunder. The trail I'd taken appeared at the edge of page two. The trail Jack had taken appeared at the edge of page four. When I folded the pages together the opposite path appeared as if a veil had been lifted from my eyes. There had been an easier path to the lake all along and I hadn't seen it. I'd thought the lows edge to the north of the lake led only to a cliff.

"Man do I feel dumb. I went through hell to get here," I said shaking my head.

"But did you see anything that way that might have been unique. Something that might have made the journey worth the extra effort?" I scoured my memories of the day. I remembered the grandeur of the sun, the vision of light and shadow across the mountains, the creatures and the birds, the peaks and the valleys. I sensed a deep caressing hand reach into my heart and touch it ever so gently in its place. Profound truths and great discoveries bled into me like a transfusion. I discovered it matters not the course of our journey. Some will find great treasures, others great wisdom and others will not learn at all. Some men will be embraced by the love of family, others will live alone. Some men will rise in stature and others serve their masters. Children will bless some men; others shall never know the joy of progeny. But the great truth that swept over me was this-no path is superior to another. All paths in life teach the same principles, only from different angles, and if your trail is flat then it is easy, but the vistas and the peaks shall forever be denied you. If your trail is treacherous and steep, it will be hard, painful and riddled with strife, but you shall know the touch of heaven and peer into the far corners of eternity that are forever denied your mollified brothers.

The ways of life are plentiful and plump. The mysterious truth is round and tender. But in the end, after cradle and grave, it will matter not. All paths are equal before the holy sun. No matter your course, in difficulty or pleasure, the greatest rewards are given to those who see the most from wherever they are privileged to stand. I placed a finger up to my eye, wiping off the small residue of a half-shed tear. "You know Jack, I just learned something extraordinarily important."

"What's that?"

"All men are miracles."

"Damn straight partner." Jack pulled out his tent and sleeping bag and set up his little fiefdom. Each step was fulfilled to the utmost degree before he moved on to another. He raised his camp with great concern and I guessed that either this was due to extreme experience or that Jack was channeling his late wife.

After settling in, Jack approached and sat beside me staring out to the stillness of the lake. Our every movement, to the smallest adjustment to the loudest belch, echoed across the water as if our noise was the sum of creation. The black rock absorbed the starlight with impunity as the penetrating light from the sky jumped into the lake and bounced back into our eyes. The light tamed the darkness and Jack drew out an ancient harmonica and positioned it gently to his lips. A tranquil noise emanated from the metal as he pushed sweet, cold air through the mouth organ. "Amazing Grace" reverberated across the vacant air and I was filled with echoes, hums, memories and camaraderie. Jack was teaching me by the waves of sound that leapt from his mouth. I closed my eyes and saw the stars in life's inner light.

Jack played for half an hour before setting the harmonica on the ground as if he had never played it, as if the sounds reverberating across the lake had been created elsewhere and transported to this spot by divine intervention. I listened to the sounds from his harmonica long after the instrument had left Jack's lips. Then, as the sounds died sweetly on the wakes and ripples I sat in silence as the small movements of critters died away and left the lake so still as to all but disappear in the moonlight. I watched Jack stare out at the water. "A penny for your thoughts?" I asked.

"You think they're worth that much?"

"Probably not, but there the only thoughts out here other than my own." I said as Jack chuckled.

"I was just thinking about sin."

"Original sin, or just sin in general?" I asked.

"Both I guess. Just what is a sin and why would we be punished for original sin if we had nothing to do with committing it. The whole gamut of sin has always kinda baffled me," Jack said then turned and faced me.

"Sin is any act not in accordance with the will of God. At least that's the Bible's definition."

"Is that what you believe?" Jack asked.

"No. Not necessarily. I believe man evolved so there could never have been one particular moment when man became man, no delineating event to divide the species. It was a graduated process punctuated at times by cataclysmic events."

"Well," Jack said, "I suppose there's the chance man wasn't created all at once, but what then is original sin and how come I have to pay for it?"

"You don't, because if there never was a delineating event then there never was a sin that was the first sin of man. We are the inheritors of genes, not sin. All sins are our own."

"I see your point, but what exactly is a sin and why do I feel guilty when I think I've committed one?"

"What I think sin is, and what another man thinks it is are in all likelihood different as one day from another. I think sin is committed when a man commits an act that is in disharmony with his own nature and the nature of man in general. Especially when the result of the act is a disintegration of progress. Man, I believe, is on earth to learn, to grow, and to experience the weight of his personal wisdom, which is inferior to that of nature."

"So you see the earth and our little life on it as a kind of school and we commit sin when we flunk a test."

"That's as good of an explanation as any. I believe the universe is a great teacher, a possessor of all truth, wisdom, and understanding. Enfolded within its spaces and its times are the dreams of eternity, the lessons of endlessness. A good example is this, when we peer out to the stars we peer back to the dawn of creation. When we spy starlight from a star a hundred million light years away we are in fact seeing light that left that star a hundred million years ago. More than that we are not reaching out into the deep of night to see this light, but are merely amplifying what is in front of our lens, a collection of photons gathered into a bowl shaped mirror and reflected back to our eyes. The knowledge of the star was here all along. The only thing that happened is we developed a sufficient awareness to bring this light from out of the darkness. So it is with all knowledge and truth. It is all around us, encircling us, dividing us, penetrating us, pouring over us. Everything there is to know is within the reach of our hands if only we possess the awareness to convey these truths into our world."

"So you're saying that if I was smart enough, and had the right technology I could know everything."

"Pretty much. You could know everything that is within the realm of possibility to know."

"I like that idea. It makes me feel like more than just a creature walking around on some lonely planet. More like a miniature god or something."

"Exactly," I stated, "If everyone is a miniature god then all is a miniature god and the only reality is that all these miniature gods form one Great God, and this Great God is the sum of all our experiences."

"Interesting concept of God I'd say. Never heard that preached in a church before."

"No, I don't suppose you ever have. Each of us must become a truth unto ourselves, a sovereign of our own life. Then each soul is a part of the greater good and each life adds something to the wealth of existence. Become yourself a religion, show me your way and I will show you mine. Together the true path will be revealed."

"Sounds a little Zen to me."

"Maybe they were on to something," I stated, "But maybe we need both east and west to guide us on the path to truth."

"I don't know. I'm just a simple man. But you could be right."

"But to get back to your original question about sin, I believe that all is progress, or at least is supposed to be progress. When a man steps back and pulls others along with him he is committing sin. Sin is any act that inhibits the soul's growth or the growth of others. It's exactly the same sin to prevent another soul from gaining an education and a life of experiences, as it is to stop your self from growing and advancing. Progress is light, all else inhabits the night."

"You might be right. Speaking of night partner, I'm tired and need to sack out. I appreciate the conversation. Maybe I'll dream about this stuff tonight and understand it in the morning?"

"Who knows but that you will not dream the great dream and know all by morning?"

"I doubt it. But here's to ya," He said as he flopped back his tent flap and went inside, "Maybe you'll have that same dream as well."

"Good night," I said with a bright smile. Jack had allowed me to think of things I rarely pondered and I sat awash in possibilities. I watched the stars for a few minutes before I retired to my black tarp tent. I listened to the stillness across the lake interrupted only on brief occasion by Jack's snoring. Then I fell asleep and found myself inside a strange, enchanted dream.

12

I fell into a deep, rested sleep. No tossing, no turning, only the calm of comfort. I began to dream sometime in the night, a dream so intense and vivid, I think of it still. It comes to me in long winter nights. Yet if pressed to explain it, I can only say that I felt it as much as dreamed it. No other dream of my life has left such a residue on my soul. In the dream I discovered myself in a frozen world. All around me ice walls and ice mountains covered the landscape like the surface of Antarctica. The cold caused my body to shake. I shivered as I watched chunks of ice plunge off the edge of the mountains. In the middle of this scene a small river flowed from left to right. Bloated chunks of ice bobbed in the chilly water, yet I was filled with an overpowering sense of peace. I heard only the sound of running water and the splash of ice into the river.

I stood for what seemed an entire day. A tiny disk of sun rose over the backs of the ice mountains and then sank again until the scene dripped in gray ooze. As the sun returned and thrust a sliver of light across the cold, a raft appeared from the left and floated uninhabited to the right as if from nowhere, returning to nowhere. This puzzled me. Even in the altered realm of dreams this seemed to have no purpose. Then another raft appeared. Sitting on the right side was my mother, as my sister sat on her left. They were clothed in the dress of ancient pioneers, bonnets and long dresses. They stared straight ahead. The blankness of their faces startled me, but as they came directly to my face my mother turned and said, "Watch the sun as it rises and sets. In it is a great mystery, sure to lead you to the hope of your life."

I struggled to reply, to gain her attention, but my mouth refused to move. And now my clothes had vanished from my dream and I stood naked, shivering in the frigid air. Without warning another raft floated in from the left. In the front sat my father in the middle and he held the same placid expression as my mother. As he passed me he said, "Time is not a thing, space is not a thing, it is all a settling of energy across an octave of eternity." At his words a blistering rush of air swept across my ears. The intensity of this exalted temperature stung my frozen ears and caused tears to run down the sides of my face.

I could not speak. I longed to wake up, to return to the warmth of my tent, but the harder I struggled the deeper I fell into the dream. I was crying hard when another raft entered from the left. In it was my best friend, a man whom I had known since I was a boy. He was as naked as I was and the raft he was sitting on had sprung a leak and was taking in water. He stared straight ahead as if unconcerned. The coldness of the water will kill him quickly, I thought. I watched as he drifted up toward my face. He turned toward me and with an expression as blank as a faceless man's he said, "I am as you are. A victim of a dream." As his leaking raft passed me I saw the bow sink into the frigid water, yet my friend did not move. I feared for his life, though I knew I was in a dream. Yet I was haunted by the prospect of his death. When the right side tipped into the water and the whole craft looked soon to follow, I dove into the water expecting to drown, but I was unable to stop myself from aiding my friend.

I braced myself for the excruciating rush of cold upon my naked body. Every muscle in my body tensed as I lifted into the air and slipped into the river. To my astonishment the water was warm. In fact it was as warm as any tropical water. I laughed at the inconsistency. It was preposterous, buffoonish, clownish, the thing of clumsy dreams. I frolicked in the water splashing imaginary mates and twisting in circles at the good fortune I'd just endured. I forgot that my friend had just been swallowed by the river and was nowhere to be found. I dove into the depths of the water and as I did a force pulled on my body from beneath. I sank and sank until I could no longer see the sky above the water. I landed on a bed of warm sand and the water vanished and the sun stood overhead, hot and full, beaming generously on my body.

People stood all about me. They watched the sun as if it might be preparing to speak. Everyone seemed happy to be on the shore. Some played along the edge of an ocean that bled into the horizon. Everyone was naked, unadorned, and full of joy. Just then the ground shook with a terrible vigor and rippled waves of thunder spread across the sand. All heads turned skyward and the sun grew bright white and formed a face with eyes, lips, nose and cheeks. The sun wrinkled its brow and spoke. "I am the sun, the giver of light and truth. All who wish to know the secrets of the universe rise up and enter my glow."

I sought to rise up. I hungered to know the riddle of existence, but a force deep inside myself prevented me from moving. Glittery diamonds appeared across the sky enticing everyone to enter the sun's domain. Myriads of people rose up and stood in the sky just beyond the touch of the sun. Many others, like myself, stood on the shore in wonder. The sun then puckered its face and turned a bright shade of crimson. His lips pursed and the sun blew out a storm harder and faster than any known on earth and all the people who were held suspended in the air were burned to cinder and their charred ashes fell back onto the sand as I stood astonished.

Then a man appeared from the inner circle of the sun, a man made of pure light, glowing white with the intensity of a supernova. He gathered the remaining people from the shore by motioning with his outstretched hands and the people, including myself, formed a large circle in the sand. He held himself suspended above us in the air and spread out his hands to the sun and said, "They, o sun, are ready for the next dream." The group of souls rose up into the air and vanished into the face of the sun. I awoke to find my body lying outside of my sleeping bag, shivering and naked.

13

In the morning, sunlight rushed into my tent so I pulled on a pair of hiking shorts and a t-shirt and reentered the world. To my astonishment Jack's tent was gone and so was Jack. Apparently, I'd overslept and the day was too far spent for Jack to hang around. On the old log by my camp stove I discovered a note with a smiley face scribbled across the top. It read-'Thanks partner for the use of the camp. I must be going along, many miles to make today. Best wishes and good fortune. I believe you are right about original sin. I've committed too many of my own sins to worry about someone else's. I think this is my last summer in the woods. I have other mountains to climb. By the way, I had a dream last night you wouldn't believe-Jack.'

I peered across the still lake and scanned for Jack, but he had vanished into the reservoir of experience we call memory. I was happy that the sun was beating hard on my shoulders; it was a defense against the cold of my dream. I packed my backpack and devoured a big breakfast of mush; aware this would be my last full day in the wilderness. Then it would be back to my other life, my life of striving, stress, family and wanting. I resolved to make this last day the best, as it would need to sustain me through never-ending hours of working boredom. I hiked to the opposite edge of the lake, said a last goodbye to the stillness, and jaunted across the meadow Jack had hiked.

The meadow was a revelation, unexpected like a sudden summer storm. Even in the early morning the meadow teemed with activity, insects of every description, bees, small birds and burrowing mammals. The meadow was reassuring after my dream. The trail was sided by aimless rows of short grasses and sparse trees that provided the appearance of an African savanna. I marveled at how easy this trail would have been to the lake. I thought about my experience on the ridges and realized I'd arrived via the trail I was preordained to travel. I'd always longed for the hard edge, the distant shore. For drifters and dreamers there are no trails, only days to load with wonder and hours that never come again.

I rediscovered the original trail and that night I camped aside a shallow lake with three other campers. I kept a watchful eye for Jack or the two schoolgirls, but I saw neither of them. I woke up on the fifth day and hard marched to the main lake by the trailhead. I stopped and watched the drifters on rubber tubes and air filled rafts. I watched trees sway in the hot August breezes. I watched children and couples frolic near the water's edge and I was glad that I'd ventured so much further into the wilderness. I'd known silence and the symphony of insects dancing on the water. I never wanted to be ordinary again. To be ordinary is to be half alive. I walked out to the trailhead and spotted my car just where I'd left it. I hopped in the front seat, drove sedately down the highway and reentered my old life. Yet I'd shed a part of my old soul and left it in the woods to sleep.

14

To the universe time is a cloak that carries history in its sleeves. The wonders of the earth are the creations of vast eons of time. There are no complex forms that materialize in the world over night. When we stare at the Grand Canyon we are not awed because it is a hole in the ground, we are awed because it is a hole that required hundreds of millions of years to form. In Oregon there is only one spot that captures a piece of this type of mystery and that is Crater Lake. Crater Lake is the only National Park in Oregon, a state well known for its unequaled state parks. The lake lies deep in the southern stretch of Oregon and is a part of the Cascade Mountains.

Approximately 7,000 years ago, according to Native American legends past down to the present day, a mountain known as Mount Mazama stood 14,000 feet high. This height would have easily made it the highest peak in Oregon. One day a gigantic explosion rocked the earth and thousands of tons of volcanic excrement thundered through the sky reaching to parts of Idaho. The top of Mount Mazama had been blown off in one cataclysmic event. What was left was a hole of monumental proportions. Imagine looking straight down into a newly formed caldera two thousand feet deep. After a brief period of cone development, which led to the formation of the only actual crater, that of Wizard Island, the great hole filled with water. It was the addition of water that gave Crater Lake its unparalleled beauty.

Sometime in the 1800's a man, legend has it, whose horse had the good sense to stop right at the edge of the caldera, discovered Crater Lake. Word spread of his discovery and Crater Lake has been a hot spot ever since. What startles the uninitiated is the extreme clarity of the water. It is possible to see over a hundred feet into the depths of Crater Lake. A lack of algae has given the lake a deep blue that strikes the eye with vigor. Little compares to the first look into the depths of a lake two thousand feet deep. The lake will more than capture your breath it will arouse the mysteries.

After a brief stint at the lodge when I was eleven, I set out to discover more of the wonder of the lake in my early forties. I prepared a tent and sleeping bag, coolers of food and a van with the roughness of a half million miles of abuse. I turned off at the Oakridge exit on Interstate Five. I traveled lazily along country roads that traversed the slippery edge of a reservoir. After several miles I entered a state park that had a waterfall as its main attraction. I was intrigued and my haunches sore so I pulled into a slot beside the restroom and hiked to the edge of the chasm. Below me a gaping hole had been punched in the world. A vast expanse lay before me, beckoning me to my death should I challenge its depths. I watched the pristine water as it poured over a hard rock surface and tumbled to the ground two hundred feet below.

Waterfalls are formed when hard rock is positioned next to softer rock during a geological upheaval. Over time the soft rock wears away leaving a large chasm where water must drop into a basin beneath. It is rare to find an ugly waterfall. There appears to be a compelling attraction even to the smallest and most mundane of falls. I stared at the falling water for twenty minutes unable to take my eyes off the perilous journey of the liquid. I wondered if the water in the calm creek above ever had an inkling of the plunge to come. I wondered if that was somehow a metaphor for our own lives as men. We skate merrily through childhood; unaware of the certain tragedy that awaits us in adulthood and even our ultimate fate as grave filler. I shook my head to rid it of gruesome prospects and returned to watching the water tumble to the pool below.

I re-gripped my senses and returned to the road. My task and mission were simple. Get to Crater Lake, learn all that is possible to absorb in one summer weekend. My van struggled up the mountainous terrain, huffing through small towns and narrow highways. Several hours later I arrived at the entrance to the park and paid a green clad woman in a wooden booth ten dollars for the privilege of looking at water. Shouldn't this be free, I thought? The lady handed me a receipt and I was unleashed to roam the park without fear of monetary retribution. I placed the receipt on my dashboard to distinguish myself from a free-loading crook.

My van crept across vistas of open lava runs. Large flows that had spewed from the earth and cooled and formed into shapes and sizes. As I rose up the narrow, pinched highway the peaks of the Cascade Mountains leaned over the top of the lava fields and appeared like temples. As I rounded a wide curve I came to a parking lot filled to capacity. All around the area there were tourists, dressed in shorts, t-shirts, sunscreen and wide hats, all of them leaning over the wooden rail at a spectacle below. I parked on the rugged highway, pushing my van far to the right, and skip-ran across the road until I stood against the rail.

I was unprepared for what lay below. Inside a ring of volcanic rock a lake had formed, so blue as to challenge the sky. It was a deep blue, born of clarity, a blue that makes one believe in other worlds. The lake was huge, nearly thirty miles in circumference and the edges of the old mountain peak stood thousands of feet above the surface of the lake. I watched a small, blue-green vessel as it darted across the water holding some two-dozen souls. An old woman blurted that it was the Forest Service boat that people could charter around the lake. I knew I had to ride it and nothing would stop me. I peered to my right and saw the lodge standing on the edge of the lake next to Garfield Peak. The lodge was rustic and old, in need of repair, but was still grand and inspiring.

I watched the boat for a few minutes as it squirted across the still water. Eventually it landed on an island that had formed in the middle of the caldera and was called Wizard Island due to its striking resemblance to a wizard's hat. The people off loaded one by one and I hungered to be among them. The island seemed mysterious and enticing. I decided to check into my campsite so, reluctantly, I hopped in the van, made a right turn past the tourist center and wound down a haphazard road until I reached the National Park Camp. I paid an additional fee

at the little wooden box and drove through eight or nine avenues
before reaching the number assigned to me.

The campsite was magnificent. Along the back of the camp a ravine,
split by a small running brook, spread across a minute valley that lent
the high altitude spot the appearance of a meadow. In the valley grew
trees and shrubs of every description and long patches of grass that
edged the babbling brook. I hungered to attack the trail down to the
water, but first I needed to set up camp for my two-night stay. I
pitched my tent at the back of the site and laid out a pale brown camp
chair. I pulled out my ancient sleeping bag, a blanket, a pillow and a
bag of clothes. Satisfied that my camp was sufficient to endure the
weekend I headed straight down the trail toward the brook.

Along the trail yellow flowers grew, short and wound in bunches.
I'd never seen any quite like them before. I slipped down the ravine
and found myself in a meadow of grass and short shrubs that lent the
illusion of Switzerland along the slopes of the Alps. I followed the
brook for half a mile. Just as the brook broke left I spied a small forest
within a forest to my right. I could not suppress my natural curiosity
long enough to retain my nonchalance to an observing crowd that had
formed along the ridge above. I sensed that they wanted to know how
to get down to where I was, but I wasn't about to tell them. It was
mine to horde.

I ventured into a thick thatch of low trees lined with short grass and
discovered a log near an opening deep inside the thicket. It looked like
an outdoor cathedral. High branches over hung the opening and low
branches formed walls and doors. I sat on the log and rested my eyes
on a narrow, but tall slit in the trees. I peered into a crevasse through
two small rocky peaks to a valley spread out like a giant blanket. I
could see from that low place a sliver of the Klamath Basin, or so I
thought. Eventually, I decided this was the case and walked further in
that direction. When I arrived near the slit unfortunately it was just
another meadow, but it was more beautiful than the one I'd just seen
so I entered through the slit in the rocks and found myself alone in a

deep, cliff lined avenue of flowers, grass, and green shrubs. I was ecstatic, high on the thin air. I will not be happier if heaven looks much the same.

Along the edges of the rock cliffs, various weeds, flowers, clumps of meadow grass and even a few creatures gave the stark, sheer cliffs the appearance of a man-made high rise. Even in nature, I thought, all the available space is put to use. The meadow itself was bounded on all sides by sheer cliffs, over two hundred feet high, and only the narrow slits at either end allowed life to enter and exit through its rocky doors. I wondered what would happen to this space if the doors were to suddenly close forever and this tiny population was isolated from the rest of the world. I was to find a measure of an answer the next day out on Wizard Island. I walked pell-mell through the opulent meadow. There were no trails, no set direction to take. When this is the case it is acceptable to wander. Perhaps this is the natural state of man, to wander, to aimlessly seek the next horizon. Somehow our man-made devices are more traps than vehicles of freedom. Despite the fact that a freeway is an open, never-ending road it habitually leads us back and forth from home to work. The road's great, unlimited possibilities too often go unused.

Then I had an electric thought. If it is true that man limits his physical boundaries by his conventions and constructions then it is true that man limits his thinking in the same way. Once men establish patterns of belief they use these conventions to squash freethinking. It requires a gargantuan leap of imagination to break free of these bounds. In fact it requires genius to do so. New thoughts must be measured by the crusty reasoning of the past before they are allowed absorption into our future. Thus mountains of free thoughts, thoughts that could revolutionize the world never see the light of day. If we would but open the doors, the entrances and the exits, to a greater scope, the world might be transformed into an Eden. Alas, it would require an end to stupidity. And since the stupid rule the world, their reign will have no end.

Late afternoon arrived as I wandered through the isolated meadow, examining every nuance. The sun fell behind the high cliff to the west and I decided to head back to camp. Along the trail I encountered a couple, dressed in hiking boots and shorts, plopping down the trail in triple time. I glanced as the dust from their rapidly placed feet hit me in the eye and I asked them a question. "You folks must be from California?" The couple did not so much as raise their heads as they passed.

"How'd you know?" The lady asked.

"Just something about Californian's I guess." I heard a faint trickle of laughter. Before I could take three steps the couple reached the bottom by the brook and were marching, heads down, making good time, as people would say, but time for what?

I arrived at camp and found that all the available spaces around me had been captured and claimed by campers of every description. Old folks in a new fifth wheel, a young couple in a dilapidated tent, a family with three young children whose mini-van was loaded beyond possibility with gear. I propped my feet up on the wooden picnic table and leaned back on my rickety camp chair. I commenced to doze for about an hour as buzzing from every conceivable human activity swirled around me. When a man is truly tired, all sound, all thoughts are only aimless noise in a universe of chaos.

I awoke to tapping on my shoulder. Startled, I waved my arms in gigantic circles to maintain a precarious balance. "Hummmph," I said to the stranger.

"Sorry to bother you, but could I borrow some coffee. I forgot to pack some and my wife is a bear if she doesn't get her caffeine." The short, thick-middled man leaned over me in a show of desperation.

"Well, I can understand that. Sure, let me get into my supplies over here and see what I can do," I said as I landed on the ground with a thud. The man offered his hand and I clasped it. He pulled me out of the chair with one sure tug. I shuffled to my van, opened the back door and scrambled to find my coffee. I found a large tin can and discovered I had more than an ample supply of fresh grounds. I scooped coffee into a smaller metal can and handed it to the stranger. He lifted it carefully in the air as if the can contained radioactive material. "By the way, my name's Allen, and yours?"

"Oh, sorry. Where's my manners. I'm Bill Jeffries, my wife Sarah and I are camped two spaces down on the left. Feel free to stop by anytime."

"Where you two from?"

"Pennsylvania."

"I love that place, a lot like Oregon."

"You've been there?"

"A year ago. It was early July and I loved the drive I took through the back roads that summer. Remember it well."

"Next time stop by and say hi, we love company."

"I will, I promise," I said and let out a small laugh.

"Thanks for the brew, you don't know what hell you've saved me from."

"Glad to help. Say, I'll stop by later, if you have a big fire going."

"We just might," Bill said as he turned and skidded back to camp, holding the small can as if his mother's ashes lay within it. I thanked the good Lord I was presently single.

15

I fixed a cold supper, too lazy to start a fire or to crank up the old camp stove. I made bologna sandwiches and washed them down with half warm beer then accented the meal with a Little Debbie pie. The campground became electrified with the bustle of late arriving campers and large gangs of roving children in search of mischief. I was thankful I'd raised my children young so that now in the twilight of my youth they were old enough to fend for themselves. The bustle soon turned into organized clamor so I hopped into my van and proceeded to the edge of the caldera to take in the sunset. I drove at a snail's pace through the camp so as not to waste a perfectly good van by slamming it against the innocent body of a child though I'd certainly come across one or two along the way that would have fit nicely flattened against my hood.

I reached the edge of the caldera just as the sun bent between two rounded peaks. It was the middle of August but by now you could sense the shrinking of the days. Autumn and its terrible winds lay sulking behind the sunshine waiting for its chance to pounce on the world. I parked next to the grand lodge and shuffled to the eastern edge to gaze at the water. I observed dozens of guests as they pulled up to the main entrance and off-loaded by the front door. I secretly longed to be among them. I hoisted myself onto the deck attached with logs to the back of the main hall. I plopped into a chair hewn from stumps bound together with tight, shrunken leather shreds. The temperature on this darkened side of the lodge was plunging fast. I tucked into a tight ball. August is the only time of year when it is warm enough to spend significant time at Crater Lake. In winter the snow piles deep and cross-country skiers and snowshoers in search of a winter treat commandeer the park.

Off to my right a soaring, slender peak lorded over the caldera from several thousand feet above. I walked to the marker on the eastern edge of the deck. The marker informed me that the protuberance was called Garfield Peak in honor of James Garfield, former President of the United States. The peak rose to 9,000 feet, two thousand feet above my head. I noticed a long, slithering trail up its body and I decided to hike to its tip the next day.

I was joined on the deck by after dinner guests. The lodge was expensive so the people to my left and right represented a privileged class. Money seemed to ooze from their bodies. I listened to endless banter about the lake, most of it horribly ill-informed and decided the privileged were a waste of my precious time. So, as the sun settled across the mountains, I trotted along the edge of the caldera and crept toward an overlook built at the edge of a sheer cliff. Along the way squirrels and chipmunks begged for their supper. I proved a grave disappointment. The deepening shadows of evening cast a black pall over the deep waters and the already deep lake appeared to end at the other side of the world.

I paused on my little excursion to notice a giant wall of volcanic rock protruding out of the water to the northeast. It intrigued me. What was it? Or rather why was it? The wall cast an even blacker shadow on the water than the rim of the caldera did. When I reached the overlook a sign pointed to the wall and proclaimed that it was called "The Phantom Ship." I thought that sounded like a reasonable name due to the fact that as the sun disappeared all together the wall vanished into the water as if it lived under the crystalline waters and rose only during the brilliance of day. I noticed, too, headlights flashing on and off around the circumference of the rim. I realized there existed a road that meandered around the entirety of the caldera. I instantly knew the way I'd take upon leaving the park.

A woman, young and eager, entered the overlook and proceeded to coo. She dripped slow, languid words from her thick mouth. It was as if she had never seen nature or anything that had so enthralled her as the lake. I couldn't resist a conversation. "You seem to really enjoy the view," I stated.

"Oh my yes. I live in New York City. I don't see things like this very often."

"I don't suppose you do. I live here in Oregon. I suppose I take it all a little for granted."

"You're lucky," she said, "I wanted to move here so badly. I wanted to come here when I finished law school. I could've started a practice out here."

"I guess Oregon's as good a place as any to practice law."

"The law's the law."

"Well Oregon is a tad different. We have a lot of strange laws and even stranger politicians. You can't even pump your own gas here."

"That's funny. Didn't know there were any states left living back in the 60's."

"You're in one I'm afraid."

"I'm sold. I love a challenge."

"Good, we can always use an infusion of new talent."

"So what are you doing up here? You and the wife sneak off for a little get away?"

"No, no wife. Had one, lost one. I'm just trying to learn about all the natural places in Oregon. Kind of a self taught nature course I guess."

"What are your plans for tomorrow. I'm here by myself, up at the lodge. I'd love an escort."

"Tomorrow I plan to take the boat ride." I said as the young lady cooed again. "Then maybe a hike up Garfield Peak."

"Could I invite myself along?"

"You know, I'm usually a bit of a loner when I'm out in the wilderness, but some company actually sounds great," I said, surprised at my own response.

"Super. I'd love that. I'm going to head back to the lodge now. Are you staying there?" She asked with intense interest.

"No. I'm staying at the campground."

"Brrrrrr. It gets so cold out here at night. I like the fire by the fire-place. Want to come and sit by it for a while. Maybe you could tell me a little about Oregon."

I remembered that I'd promised myself a campfire, but she seemed earnest and cute and a bit hard to resist, though she was only three or four years older than my own daughters, so I agreed. We paced toward the lodge passing several other sightseers along the way. I told her about Oregon, the best places to visit, the best of our history as I could remember it. She in turn informed me about New York. What it was like to live near millions of people. What the city sounded and looked like. I was as enthralled by her descriptions as she was by mine.

By the time we reached the hall with the fireplace I was shaking from the cold. Even in mid-August the temperature can plunge below freezing. Snow in July is commonplace. She had wrapped up in a thick, warm coat and tossed it aside as we entered the warm hall. I located two seats at the edge of the grand fireplace that bristled and crackled with an infusion of fresh logs. We sat and a lady walked by and asked if would like hot chocolate from the dining hall. I almost fell down and worshipped her.

"I never introduced myself. I'm Allen Scarbrough from Dallas, Oregon. I'm a salesman by trade, but a dreamer by profession." She laughed and looked into the roaring fire.

"My name's Candice. You already know I'm a law student from New York."

"Nice to meet you Candice. Pardon my asking but this seems like a big, expensive trip for a student."

"It is, my parents paid for it. I come from money. I didn't want to tell you that because you look like someone who doesn't care for the rich. If I told you my last name you'd have heard of my family."

"That's okay, first names are good enough for me. So you're a real honest to God blueblood?"

"The bluest of the blue. But it's not as great as people think. I was born into it, didn't have a choice. Sometimes I long for a simpler way of life. I suppose that's why I came out here."

"Well, dang it, I'm determined now to show you around. I want you to go back to New York and sing Oregon's praises. Maybe I'll charge a finders fee and become a blueblood like yourself." Candice mockingly slapped me across the face.

"Be careful what you wish for, you just might get it."

The lady returned with our cocoa and I guzzled mine, causing my throat to burn raw. However, the hot liquid felt devilishly good as it slid to the bottom of my stomach. Candice watched me with quiet amusement. We chatted for hours about the natural wonders of Oregon, the meaning of life, the novels of Tolstoy. She was an educated young woman and I couldn't help but adore her. I seemed to be filling some profound unfilled need in her soul. She dangled on my every word. It made me feel like an expert on the world, and compared to her I probably was. Her light gold hair flowed from side to side, her bright eyes taking in the room, then me, then the room, and then her hands. She was a bright girl and except for her age, which I guessed to be twenty-three I would have invited myself to her room. As the hour approached 11p.m. she looked straight into my eyes.

"I'm dead tired. It's time for bed. It's such a long way back to the camp. Why don't you come up with me and go back in the morning?" I knew better, but she had asked with such total honesty, with such total hunger in her eyes that I melted and gave in to her. At these critical moments in a single man's life he doesn't know if the night is a prelude to regret or the entrance to a bright new chamber of memory. I walked her up to her room. It was the presidential suite.

We found each other in the dark, before she could switch on the lights. The moon glowed through the window and glittered across the water visible beneath us. She pressed into me, gave herself to me. I'd never experienced such a deep and unrealized need. Candice was a melting candle rushing not to be put out before all her light was used up. I made love to her. She was young and clumsy, but I so adored her I made love to her twice. In the morning a golden breakfast appeared at our door. Candace glowed.

After devouring the fruit I drove back to camp. When I arrived the tent was still there, but the whole scene looked surreal as if some other poor slob was unlucky enough to dwell there. I changed into shorts and light hiking boots, grabbed my camera and drove straight back to the lodge to meet up with Candice. I pulled in front of the main door and Candice leapt out of her hiding spot and lunged toward the van. I leaned over and let her in. She struggled into the high seat and smiled.

"I'm ready for adventure Allen. Fire it up and roll it out."

"All right then, let's go boating." I drove around the first quarter of the lake encountering few cars in the still early hours of Saturday. Candice and I were hoping to make the first boat ride of the day at 9a.m. and see the lake in its first slivers of daylight. I found the new parking lot across the road from the trail to the boats and parked alongside two RV's. Candice discovered a trailer dispensing fresh coffee and soon she gripped a large latte in her delicate hands. This was a decision she would soon come to regret. It reminded me of just how young she was.

After hustling Candice to drink fast we walked across the road to the trailhead. A warning sign that pregnant women and people with a variety of heart troubles should not attempt the trail framed the starting point. I wondered to myself why it was rated so difficult. The boat landing looked so near to us from the top of the caldera. Nevertheless, we began a slow march down to the lake. Through the openings in the trees we saw the morning sun as it skipped across the surface of the calm water. The smell of fresh forest, the thin air, the sound of our feet crunching in the volcanic gravel filled me with bliss. Candice smiled and I sensed she was having a private experience I wasn't privy to. She appeared younger in the morning light. The soft shadows on her golden hair leeched across her face and gave her mouth and nose the qualities of childhood. I wondered if she was too young. I thought I should leave her after the boat ride, but then I caught a glance of her feminine form as she turned a switchback on the trail and I was reminded that this was no girl, but a woman capable of her own decisions.

The trail flopped back and forth in a struggle to keep hikers on an even keel. We were hiking straight down the edge of the caldera, only the constant snapping back and forth prevented our tumbling into the lake. About twenty minutes later we arrived at the boat dock to find that twenty-two others had preceded us. I jumped to the ticket window and bought the last two tickets for the morning ride. Then we waited, and waited. At last a boat pulled up to the dock and preparations were made for boarding. I skipped over to the edge of the lake and looked down into the clear blue water. I could see the bottom. I'd never seen water so clear. Then a sense of panic swept over me. The true depth of the lake manifested itself to my mind and I realized a plummeting body would float almost two thousand feet down before touching bottom. I swallowed my fear and steadied Candice as she stepped into the boat.

"Don't fall overboard. It's a long way to the bottom," I said with a chuckle. Candice peered over the edge of the boat and several creases formed on her forehead. She sat, pensive, as the boat drew away from the sanctuary of the dock. A minute later the promise of the bottom of the lake vanished and all that we could see was the blue water of the surface and the black dankness of the bottom. I gripped the edge of the boat and Candice gripped me.

A park ranger, Tom, was the designated tour guide. As the boat sped across the cool water, splaying mist into faces, Tom discoursed on the history of the lake. But all I could think about was the stupendous proportions of the caldera. What had seemed miniscule from above now appeared gigantic. From the road Garfield Peak appears as a mere bump above the caldera, but on the water the peak seemed thousands of feet high. As we scuttled the western edge of the lake a protruding bump appeared on our right. Tom told a tall tale about the bump being the neck of a great warrior-god whose head had fallen into the water and become Wizard Island.

I was enjoying the splendor of the early morning, the spray of mist on my face, the feel of Candice in my arms and the thought of skimming across a lake half a mile deep when out of the blue Wizard Island appeared as the boat made a sharp right. It was huge compared to the boat. We docked and off loaded by the edge of a fresh trail. Excitement rushed through me as I thought about hiking to the top of the crater and peering down. I pulled Candice out of the boat and she winced in pain. "What's wrong?" I asked.

"Pee, bad," she replied.

"No toilets darling dear. Shoulda thought of that before we left." I said like a scolding parent and with the age difference between us already a sore spot I quickly recouped my dignity. "That's okay, happens to us all. Maybe we'll find a big bush up the trail." Candice stepped to my side as we started up the steep trail to the top of Wizard Island.

Tom asked us to take a look at the wildlife and see if we noticed any differences between the wildlife on the island and that in the park, and if we found any differences to try and figure out how they came about. I accepted the challenge. As we hiked the rocky hillside grew more open, less covered by tall trees and thick shrubbery. Candice discovered a huge boulder and yanked on my sleeve. I nodded and she disappeared behind the boulder to take care of business. I stood and gazed toward the lodge when a little snake slithered across my feet. It was black with a red stripe on its back. The only other snake I'd seen at the park had a yellow stripe on its back. I noted the difference. Candice appeared from behind the boulder, a look of solemn relief on her pretty face. I smiled. "Whew," she said, "That felt good."

"Better than last night?" I asked.

"No way." We continued our climb as the rising temperature caused the first sweat of the day to roll off our heads and down our necks. I was reminded I was hiking at altitude. The water was at about 6,500 feet, high enough to cause me to draw in huge quantities of air to satisfy my ever-increasing need. Candice was still breathing through her nose.

We plodded up the twisting trail as some of our boating group passed us. I felt I was slowing us up so I tried to look youthful by striding boldly from that point forward. I almost died in the attempt. Candice kept pace no matter how slow or fast I went. It was a fact that endeared her to me. At last, as we made our final twist, the top of the crater appeared. About eight of our group already stood around the hole in the world. I walked up to the edge and peered down. The hole was round and deep and covered in reddish colors left over from its lava spewing days. The island had formed after the cataclysmic event in a final push of lava out of the tube that had formed below.

"Wow," Candice said as she peered into the crater. I wanted to mock her, but my better senses got hold of me. "How come this crater formed inside the other one?" She asked. A bald, thick-lenses man walked over and recanted the whole history of the lake, which we had already heard before, but Candice was too polite to stop him. I stopped listening and stared across the lake at the Phantom Ship. From the road it had appeared as a small protruding wall of rock, but from the island it looked as tall as a skyscraper. When the man finished, Candice thanked him and I nodded.

"Please don't do that again," I whispered.

"I won't. I forgot you already told me the story. I just forgot. I'm sorry," she said, as her eyes grew moist around the edges.

"Apology accepted," I replied then squeezed her hard around the shoulders and planted a kiss on her salty forehead. She nudged her head into my chest and I stroked her long hair.

I looked at my watch and realized we had just enough time to get back to the boat. I said, "Ten minutes to shove off," loud enough for all to hear and the remaining passengers all started down the trail in a voiceless herd. Candice and I were last in line and we kissed all the way to the dock. Unfortunately, two kids had plopped themselves into our seats and the only two left were at the front next to ranger Tom. I assisted Candice into the boat and sat near Tom, so close in fact I could smell the leather from his new boots. The boat pushed off and as we drifted into the main body of the lake Tom quizzed us on our nature hike.

"Did anyone notice any differences on the island?" Tom asked. Two teenagers with tattoos mentioned that the squirrels on the island had different markings. Tom acknowledged them and said that was true. Then I mentioned the snakes and Tom smiled. "That's good," he stated, " Now why would there be differences?" A few theories were bandied about. My favorite was the floating log theory. According to this theory several of the animals floated out to the island on large logs. I knew that wasn't right, but I loved the show of imagination. I'd seen from the lodge that on the south side of the island a slightly submerged bridge connected the island to the caldera. The lake had filled slowly, over hundreds of years. The animals had simply walked out to the island and then were cut off from the mainland when water sealed off their escape route. I recanted the tale to Tom who smiled and repeated my words to the rest of the boat over his painfully loud bullhorn. "Your so smart," Candice cooed. I said nothing. Silence is often the wisest thing you can say.

The boat sped across the lake, struggling to make time in the sun-baked morning. A log, old and weathered drifted near the boat and Tom called it 'the old man of the lake'. It had fallen into the lake over a hundred years ago and stood upright due to its unusual properties. Candice popped out a disposable camera from her bag and snapped a quick picture. As we drifted near the lodge we saw people, ant-like, striding along the path above our heads. Tom encouraged us to wave and so we did. About fifteen minutes later the Phantom Ship came into view. According to Tom it was almost nineteen hundred feet tall. I remembered how insignificant it had looked along the rim. Candice began another slurry of snapshots.

As we passed near the monolithic ship we passed over some of the deepest parts of the lake. The blackness of the depths caused me to shutter. I imagined an ignominious death plummeting to the volcanic bottom never to be seen again. The thought made graves seem friendly by comparison. We circled the ship and Candice, awestruck, snapped and snapped. I sat as we circled and thought again how it is that complexity is a byproduct of time. The true glories of this earth are formed by the infusion of eons into the fabric of space. Men are still sprouts sitting in the morning dew awaiting the full-grown sun to craft them into trees. Man is yet a child of the dawn. We live near the surface of an uncommon star. Our sun will shine for only a few billion years. If life can evolve here, how much greater are the odds of it forming near red dwarf stars that will shine for a trillion years. Man has a destiny in space. If we do not pursue the goal of colonizing other worlds, we will soon have an end. And not just the death of our species, but the fiery end to all remembrance of our ever having existed. We are little buds floating on a crumb of dust. Earth is no more our eternal home than was the sea the final destination of life.

Candice grabbed my hand as we sped away from the ship and headed toward a rendezvous with the dock. "Thanks for bringing me along. This is such a romantic place."

"Thanks for the company. You may be young, my dear, but you have the presence of an 'old soul.'"

"Perhaps we met in another life?"

"Let's not get into that. I'm a realist. I only dream about what is possible."

"I think it was ancient Egypt."

"Yea, I was King Tut and you were Nefertiti. Why is no one ever a slave or a house maid in these scenarios?"

"Who wants to remember a life like that?"

"Exactly." The boat drifted along the northern edge of the caldera and as the morning bled into the heat of day we tied up back at the dock. Candice and I took a long last look at the lake from the shore.

We smiled at each other and started the long march to the top of the trail. I was huffing in no time as Candice walked slowly so as not to embarrass me. I hadn't noticed the altitude on the way down, but now, as I took painful step after painful step, the thin air burned into my lungs. Candice, a full eighty pounds lighter, skipped up the trail as I sweated and strained. I felt old, too old to be running with a twenty-three year old. I felt seventy and was sure I looked it too.

Candice was sweet and held her hand against my back to nudge me forward. I was sure she would run from me as soon as I reached the trailhead. I was sure she had just grasped what an old geezer she had hooked. I finally had to relax on a bench provided by the park service. Several of our boat mates passed us by. I pretended to be sightseeing to avoid the truth that I was out of shape. After I recharged my lungs and regained control of my breathing I marched in steady, stuttering steps. My body settled into a rhythm and I was able to go at a straight and reliable pace. Candice was patient, but I was certain of being dumped soon. Not that I had an aversion to being alone, I just preferred aloof-ness when it was my personal choice and not the consensus of all around me.

After all the fluids had sweated from my body we reached the top of the trail and I ran to the snack shack and ordered a giant cola after stepping in front of a hesitant kid. Candice chastised me for not order-ing water, but I brushed her off. I wanted the largest cola made. I guz-zled the hapless fluid through a straw, making raucous sucking noises that echoed through the parking lot. Candice took it all in stride never saying a negative word. I expected her to run any minute.

"You're cute, you know that?" She cooed.

"So are you, and sweet as candy." And I meant it. The most surpris-ing moments in life are those when the actions of others contradict the notions in our heads. These moments keep us alive, keep the pull of death from our soul. If not for the love of life we find in others we would not understand the love that labors in ourselves. Candice was a pretty girl, blonde and button-nosed, but I stared into her heart and found a guileless angel there.

"We need to eat and get started up Garfield Peak if we want to get that in today," Candice said. I ached in every fiber of my being, but I hungered to be near her and to be strong in her eyes. I ached only to lie down and take a nap, but the thought of Candice leaving me for younger pastures devoured my reluctance. I was headed into suffering beyond agony and all for the admiration of a woman. So what else is new?

"All right sweetie pie, let's try to get by, by eating a burger and fry, and trying not to die, until we try, to climb to a peak nearby, and see a view that'll make you cry."

"What?" Candice burst into laughter, uncontrollable, irrepressible, and that's when she regretted her morning coffee indulgence. A wet spot formed along the inner edge of her shorts. She had peed her pants. Now I was the one in position to be sweet. I ran to the van and pulled out a sweatshirt and put it around her waist and led her to the bathroom. She was crying now and hurt. I put my arm around her and pushed her into the port-a-potty. I heard sobbing as it leached from the plastic box.

A couple of minutes passed into half an hour. I pleaded with Candice to come out, but she wouldn't stop crying. "Sweetie, I've seen it all. Trust me, you do not see four children being born without seeing some strange stuff. Let's go back to the lodge and get you changed and fed." I was aware that I sounded like a father.

"I can't look you in the eye. I was trying so hard to act grown up around you. But sometimes I feel like I'm still a little girl."

"Sweetie, come on out and let's get moving. The day's a wastin'." I pushed open the unlocked door and stepped inside. Candice looked deep into my eyes as tears ran down both sides of her face. I pulled her up from the toilet seat and pulled up her soaking wet pants and she melted into my arms. "You see Candice, I don't care about what you did. We are all half grown up and half child. When you pushed me up the trail and stayed with me I felt old, too old. All of us are only a thin veneer of civilization pasted onto a body of clay. Don't cry, I think you're very grown up." After several minutes of reduced sobbing Candice pushed me out the door and we hopped into my van, she sitting on a towel, and headed back to the lodge.

16

When we arrived I snatched her key and hustled to her room and found a clean pair of shorts by her bed. I grabbed them and she changed in the back of my van so no one would notice her wet shorts. We went to her room and she showered while I read Newsweek. Then an idea struck me. If I snuck into the shower with her and made her feel like a woman again she would feel better and the day wouldn't be wasted. I stripped and entered the bathroom. Candice was scrubbing to remove the residue of shame from her body. I pulled back the curtain and startled her. I stepped into the square shower and held and kissed her. We made love as water rained on our bodies. Candice emerged from the shower renewed and smiling. I'd saved a soul, a sweet soul worth saving and received intense pleasure from the experience. Win win, if ever there was such a beast. Candice and I, clean and relaxed, walked through the lobby like newlyweds on their honeymoon. I was young again, ready to hike peaks and see visions. That feeling lasted about thirty paces up the steep slope of Garfield Peak.

Garfield Peak is the last reminder that a great mountain once inhabited this landscape. I tried to visualize Mount Mazama as it must have looked 7,000 years ago. I wished that it were still there even though an even greater beauty had replaced it. This idea struck me as somehow wound into the fabric of the world. We humans are always saddened by the loss of anything in this life that we have loved, or liked, or engaged in, as if what must follow must be less than what had been. However, the truth of the world is that all is prelude. Out amid the great vistas of time, in the future beyond even the scope of the last man, there will be wonders and dreams beyond what we have imagined, or indeed can imagine. The last tomorrow will render even the bounds of time and space as only the linchpin of a greater reality.

Candace stood by the trailhead that overlooked the peak with wide eyes and pulsing blood. She was eager, fervent, and impatient to hike the tall peak and gaze into the Klamath Basin to the south, to peer across the Cascades and to stare at the water below. I couldn't get her to stop to allow myself to get mentally prepared. She dragged me up the first leg to a plateau where I stopped and discovered that all of my limbs were weighty, futile and old. The temporary relief of the shower gave way to the harshness of the altitude, the steepness of the trail and the heady smell of innumerable yellow plants. Candice was full of life, energy and adventure, I had no choice but to swallow hard, grit my teeth and step one foot forward at a time.

As we climbed, the lodge grew smaller and less significant. From the road the lodge appears massive, elevated and aloof, but from the heights a man could see that the lodge was miniscule compared to the stupendous proportions of the caldera. As we climbed the lodge shrunk as it was fitted among the mountains, lava flows, forests and cinder cones around us. This struck me as much how man has discovered his place in the cosmos. First we learn we are circling the sun and not the other way around, then that we are part of an ordinary galaxy, which is only one among billions, and then we discover that perhaps we are not even in the only universe. Man shrinks in importance the more knowledge he gains, what does that tell you about importance? I think it tells us that everything is important and insignificant depending on our current point of view. How egalitarian, I thought, that the universe plays no favorites.

Candice chattered about every new discovery while I struggled to keep enough air in my lungs to stay upright. I nodded my head and grunted whenever possible to give her the illusion I was listening. Every pore of her body was electrified, her face glowed and her eyes glistened. Over time several couples and two families passed us on the way down. They were not smiling, but looked tired, beat up, and hungry for the lodge. I wanted to cry, I mean sit down and ball my eyes out. What, I asked myself, am I doing trying to hike up this peak. I wanted to run back down and take up a soft seat on the deck and be served rum and cokes all afternoon, but I took one look into Candice's face and realized the burden of being a man. To get sex we posture and parade until the world wears us away. We accept early death and infirmity in order to appear to females as a strong and virile force of nature, when all we really want to do is sit by a warm fire and talk of peaceful things. I started to break and run, a rush of thoughts flooding my mind, but before I could execute my plan I glanced at Candace and saw how lovely she was, how eager and how willing to please me and all the sagacity and wisdom of forty years evaporated into a puddle the size of a pea and I smiled and followed her every step.

A half hour later we had managed to rise high enough to see the Klamath Basin to the south. The basin is a vast plain of flat land and pasture that reaches to the border of California. The clarity of the air and the intensity of the sunlight offered a clear view spanning at least a hundred miles. The 25,000 or so miles of the earth's circumference seemed at that moment as far around as a trip to the moon. We modern men always think of the world as overpopulated, but the truth is the entirety of humanity could stand shoulder to shoulder in a space of twenty miles square. What we truly lack is imagination. When men learn to fully exploit the resources of their minds, then, and only then, will the full resources of the earth be put to our use. Hunger, poverty, disease, and overpopulation are not problems indigenous to the world, but are the creations of limited understanding. In the future, when men are wiser, the solutions to these problems will leap out of the earth and swallow the suffering of man. It is only our lack of vision that prohibits their discovery.

Candice decided to stop and snap a few pictures. I was filled with rapturous joy. The rest gave my lungs time to catch up to the oxygen debt I'd been running. I sucked in huge volumes of atmosphere and soon my extremities tingled with the glow of thin, clean air. I was enjoying the hike at last. "Allen, how far do you think we'll be able to see once we reach the top?" Candice asked with a camera to her face.

"I suppose a hundred miles all the way around. Something like that, I didn't actually bring a measuring tape."

"Stop being so smart-alecky, I just wanted to know."

"It'll be far, very far."

"Thanks hon. I could have said that myself." I tried to deflect Candice's minor irritation by taking five steps up the trail and standing arms akimbo as if waiting for her, as if I was the driving force behind this adventure. It worked. Candice saw me and said, "I'm sorry, I don't want to hold us up. Be right there." In one minute I'd swung from foolish old man to world conquering hero. Such are the fickle fortunes of politicians and generals. All men of power live by their talent to move men, or die by their inaction.

The last stretch of the trail grew steeper as the air stretched to razor thinness. I gulped large thundering wisps of air. Sweat had drenched my clothes as the heat of the early afternoon rained on our heads. I was tired, abused, manhandled and mad. Candice had been walking in front of me for the last fifteen minutes so she couldn't see the near death experience I was living. I kept quiet and struggled to breath like a dying hyena. At last, the trail flattened and the top of Garfield Peak appeared around a last corner of rocks and I almost wept. Candice skipped ahead to the rock and rested at the tip, which enabled me to suck in enough air to recover some sense of male dignity.

I reached the peak and a vista as grand as any I have ever seen encompassed me. I could detect the far peaks of the Cascades, the endless pastures of the Klamath Basin, the tip of Mount Shasta, the circumference of Crater Lake Park and the wonders of half a state in one dazzling view. Candice tossed from side to side striving to capture the full pleasure of the scene. "Man, I've never seen anything like this before. What a sight. Come look!" She beckoned. I strutted toward her and stared at the lake. A deep, penetrating blue body of water reflected into my eyes. I watched light waves ripple across the surface and cloud patterns as they altered the color of the water. It was a perfect sight, a clamoring halleluiah, a vibratory hymn, an electric prayer.

"My God, what a wonder this place is. Thank goodness I came. I love you for making me come here today," I said and then immediately withdrew the word love. "I mean I'm happy you wanted to come here with me."

"I knew what you meant."

"No, I take it back again. I meant love. Why can't a man love a woman and not have it mean romantic love?"

"So you don't love me romantically?"

"I love being romantic with you, but we just met and I'm leaving tomorrow."

"Good, just checking to see if your head was on straight."

"Since when has any man's head been on straight where a woman is concerned?" I stated as Candice laughed. She spread out her arms and spun in tight circles as she gazed at the changing clouds overhead.

"Look. A clown face, and there's an elephant, and there's an angel," she said pointing to globs of clouds as she spun. Then she stopped and landed in my arms. She planted a bid, sloppy kiss on my lips. "I like you a lot."

"Do you like me, or like-like me," I said to tease her.

"Come on, I'm not that young."

"No you're not, your old as time."

"Really, then how old does that make you?"

"We're the same age, my dear, all beings are from before the world was made."

"You sure about that?"

"Yep. Intelligence is the fundamental property of the universe. Intelligence, or the light of our souls, has always been, and will always be. We are eternal."

"Then maybe we met in another life?"

"Shhhhhh," I said placing a finger on her full lips. "No more of that." Candice rubbed her hands over my chest then slipped out of my arms and stood near the sheerest edge of the cliff.

"What if I fell right now?"

"You'd be crushed into a thousand tiny slivers of flesh."

"Oh."

"Sweetie, let's head down now and get some supper. I could eat half a cow."

"All right. Just a few more minutes." She stared at the views from every angle sucking them in as if they could be brought into her soul like a liquid. I watched her touch each scene with her eyes and then burn them into her memory as if she was certain she would never see these grand vistas again. I bathed her body in light pulled from the sun, and for a moment, she illuminated the whole of the world.

17

We slapped our feet as we descended from the peak and Candice thought it was a game, but the truth was I couldn't raise my feet high enough to prevent the sound. When we reached the lodge I collapsed into a chair on the back deck and couldn't be moved for almost an hour. Candice amused herself by feeding the squirrels that lived an exquisite life on the generosity of tourists. I slipped in and out of dreams. My body commandeered my mind and I was forced to think whatever my laboring body demanded. Each time I struggled to stand my legs would quiver and shake until I was forced to sit back down. I downed three ice teas and a small jug of water before I could take possession of my body for the purposes of movement. Candice came to my side and rubbed my back and legs and to tell you the honest truth it felt better than sex.

By the greatest of human efforts I made the long walk to the dining hall, wishing to God that I could just lie down and die. I ordered a thick steak and piles of potatoes as Candice ordered a delicate plate of salad and fresh, hot bread. I downed two quick beers and the pain subsided to the point I could converse coherently.

"Tonight, darling dear, you are camping with me out under the stars. I have a tent and one sleeping bag. That's all we'll need."

"Okay, that sounds fun. I've never camped before."

"Never?"

"Nope. Never. My family was the jet to Paris type."

"My family was the tent and take out type." Candice giggled and looked away as if remembering a lost piece of time. I slurped my steaming clam chowder and thought of my own lost years. My family was now a splintered fraction of what it had once been, everyone having drifted into the years. I felt alone for the first time on my trip and wondered if I was doomed to die in a nursing home as elderly nurses fretted that the old man was all alone in the world. I reached out and clasped Candice's delicate hand and she smiled into my heart. It wasn't that I loved her in any real sense, or that I thought her wise or sophisticated, that made me long to be with her, but perhaps it was what she lacked that attracted me. She lacked the bitterness of age, the narrow minded-ness of failure, the collapse of free thought that comes with great wealth. She was new and freshly touching the world.

I ate my steak, cutting bites of meat with anal precision. Candice finished before me and watched as I ate every last piece of food near my hands. We exited to Candice's room and I stared out the window as she packed an overnight bag for what was, to her, a grand adventure. I looked forward to sleeping on the hard ground about as I would the second coming of the black plague. What she needed was a change of clothes and perhaps a comb and toothbrush what she took was enough supplies for a safari in Kenya. I grabbed the stuffed bag and hauled it down two flights of stairs, wincing in pain. We reached the van and I struggled to hoist the black Gucci bag into the back. I pretended that it required little effort while I bit down hard on my teeth.

I fired up the old beast and after three coughs and huffs the engine turned smooth and clean. I turned left at the crossroads toward the campground. I wondered if Candice had the stomach for camping. Perhaps, I thought, I was about to kill some of the young lady's enthu-siasm for adventure. I waved to the green-clad lady in the wooden booth and Candice waved too as if she thought it was required. I found my camp near the back and parked as close as possible to the picnic table in order to shorten the distance I'd have to haul the heavy bag. Candice jumped out and scouted the area. She was clearly taken with the canyon at the rear.

"My God, this is wonderful Allen. You should have told me it was so beautiful here."

"I thought I did."

"No way. I would have made you bring me here sooner if I would've known."

"Sorry, but you're here now." I said and then opened the back doors of the van and pulled out the bag, setting it on the table with great care.

"I want to explore down the canyon," Candice stated as if requesting a simple thing.

"I did that yesterday. I'll pass."

"Oh, come on babe," she cooed. I melted even though the thought of hiking one more step seemed impossible and fraught with the certainty of death. I swallowed and took the first step toward the trail when a stroke of genius popped into my head. I tripped and stumbled about ten feet down the trail. Candice ran back and pulled me to my feet. She braced me by standing under my left arm and led me tenderly back to my camp chair near the fire pit. "I think we'll have to pass on the hike. Let me get some rubbing lotion from my bag." She walked to her bag and pulled out a small first aid kit. She dabbed disinfectant over the wide wound on my left knee and then rubbed my legs with hot lotion that burned deliciously as I laid back and closed my eyes.

In fact the brilliance of my strategy was that Candice, wanting a fire, went over to the neighbors and got the old man to come over and start one for us. I sat and looked miserable as the old man placed sticks and lit them with great precision. I thanked him and Candice tended the fledgling fire as I drank another beer she brought me from the cooler. I thought, I can be so damn smart sometimes. Candice unpacked her bag and placed several items in the tent. I hoped there would be enough room left for the both of us. As I formed my lips around my second beer a familiar voice echoed from behind me. "Hey neighbor, startin' the party a little early I see. Sarah and I came over last night and no one was home."

"Hey Bill. Grab a seat on the table. I'm injured, fell down the trail a ways so taking some liquid medication." Bill smiled. "Actually I met a young lady up by the lodge and stayed in her room last night." Bill came over and gave me a high five.

"Excellent," he stated, then Candice appeared from the tent and her young age startled Bill. "Very, very excellent. Say Sarah and I wanted to invite you to the overlook tonight to watch the meteor shower. We'll drive so I think you'd be able to make it."

"What do you say Candice. Want to go watch the stars tonight?"

"Yes. Fantastic. I wanted to do that last night, but we fell asleep," Candice replied and then walked behind me and rubbed my neck.

"Candice, this is Bill. I met him Friday night."

"How are you Bill? It's nice to meet you," Candice said, smiling.

"Very nice to meet you too," Bill said, as he looked her up and down. It was clear that Bill would be living vicariously through me for the evening. I felt a sense of pride that I'd somehow become the idol of a man my own age. "Well look old buddy. I'm goin' to go and help fix supper. We'll pick you guys up at eight."

"Sounds like a plan Stan. Be here at eight and don't be late."

"Later Gator," Bill said as he hopped off the table and skipped across the neighbor's campsite to his own.

"Do all Oregonians talk like you two goofballs?" Candice asked.

"Yep. It's a secret language, kinda like the Gypsies. Hang around a while and maybe I'll teach it to you."

"No way. I'll keep my eastern accent thank you sir."

I coaxed a third beer out of the cooler by persuading Candice that the cold liquid was making me feel better. Afterwards she decided to go to the nature show put on by the forest rangers. I begged off due to injury and she returned with a head full of new information that she couldn't wait to tell me. I listened with the half of my brain still functioning as she poured out a great deal of information, all of which I already knew.

Near eight Bill and his wife Sarah arrived in their Suburban. Sarah was huge. I don't mean fat or heavy, I mean huge. Bill helped her out of the Suburban as if he was assisting a princess out of a carriage. He appeared unaware of her enormous size. "Hey old man. How's the appendages?"

"Still attached, but sore as hell." Candice came over by the campfire and introduced herself. Sarah and Candice began a discourse on the wonders of Oregon while Bill and I chatted about his car.

"How do ya like the old beast?" I asked.

"Gas guzzler, but good on the road," Bill replied. I watched Candice for any sign that she was getting bored, but she was talking animatedly, swinging her arms in wild gestures as Sarah giggled. Finally, Candice and Sarah reached a breathing point and I interjected that it was time to get moving if we wanted to see the best of the meteor shower. Bill hauled Sarah into her seat as Candice and I hopped into the back. He switched on the beast and it rumbled through camp. A Sherman tank would have been quieter.

We reached the overlook and found it vacant. Either the rest of humanity was unaware or just plain disinterested in meteors. Bill parked in the middle of two spaces and Candice and I jumped out as Bill hoisted Sarah from the rig. We spread an old blanket out on the very edge of the caldera and I fetched the cooler out of the back of the car and passed cold beers to everyone. It was chilly, but Bill brought four blankets out of the Suburban and each of us wrapped up tight. Candice squeezed as close to me as possible while Bill and Sarah sat far apart. I chalked this up to undo familiarity.

The sky was full of stars in the clear night as a soft, reflected glow shimmered over the area. I could see the shadows of everything, but the substance of nothing. We were like the inhabitants of Plato's cave. We saw shadows and thought they were real. Sarah leaned over and fell onto her back. So to avoid embarrassment Bill also fell backwards and Candice and I did likewise. The four of us lie under the stars and let light enter us, caress us, and entertain us. The sky was so white it looked like a painter had sprayed white paint on a black wall. The moon was bright, still. Then it began and I will never forget it.

"Look, look, five meteors just fell over my left shoulder," Sarah said.

"There's three more," Candice cooed. Within five minutes at least a hundred meteors dashed across the crystalline sky frying in the atmosphere to formless cinder. It was better than fireworks. I grabbed Candice's hand and pointed toward each meteor I saw and she did likewise to me. It was amazing that the sky could feel so alive, that something that appeared a dark and empty space could be so animated, as if out of a sea of darkness life was jumping into the world.

"Holy moly, what a scene!" Bill shouted. His voice carried over the empty air and landed somewhere on the side of a cliff.

"Thanks for gettin' us to come here Bill, really special, spectacular," I stated.

"Yes, thank you," Candice added.

"My pleasure, kids." Just then Sarah farted. Not the quaint and dainty fart of an unsuspecting lady, but the deep guttural barbarity of a truck driver. The smell passed over my nostrils and my stomach crept into my esophagus. Bill, again to avoid embarrassment, laughed it off. "Whew, that must have felt good." Sarah lay still on the blanket and we ignored her as best as possible. What Bill saw in this woman I never discerned. She was lazy and uncouth and of precious little value to humanity, but he loved her for reasons only a god could fathom and treated her with the utmost respect and courtesy. It seemed to me that if Bill could find a way to love Sarah then all men had the capacity to love one another. Claims of our differences are all a farce, a stupid trick played on us by tyrants. If we desire love strong enough it is ours. The faults of the world lay within our own hearts. Laying hatred on the doorstep of deity is a vain occupation. It will always be returned unopened.

For more than an hour meteors streaked across the night sky looking like pins of fire burning the fabric of space. We didn't speak. Words seemed small and inadequate to describe the joy we felt in so glorious a moment. Then in an instant it was over. The sky fell silent and ordinary. We gathered up and Bill dropped Candice and I back at camp. I thanked him profusely for the ride and the star show, but what

I truly gained from him I never spoke out loud. From Bill I learned what love was. Love, as it relates to humanity, contains the seed of foolishness. If men are not willing to appear foolish we cannot learn to love each other. The wisest act of preservation man can attain is to love himself; therefore to love all of mankind requires a foolish disposition. All the greatest men of earth have been fools, after they first cast aside their morbid and fruitless wisdom.

Candice and I huddled close in the lone sleeping bag. The cool night turned frigid and the thinness of the bag soon became apparent. Candice and I were naked. I rubbed my hands up and down her body and she forced me on top of her. I was so exhausted I could barely move. I'd already made love to her that morning, so for the first and only time in my life I faked an orgasm. It is easy to do when your partner is young and unsuspecting. Besides, Bill had taught me that love is foolishness. I felt foolish, but bathed in love. I fell asleep holding Candice, happier than I'd been in years.

18

In the morning I awoke to the singing of birds and the shuffle of Candice's feet near the campfire. I poked my head out and Candice stood bending over a small fire struggling to heat a pot of coffee. I threw on an old sweatshirt and jeans and stumbled out of the tent. "Good morning, Mary Sunshine. You're sure bright and chipper this morning. And cooking no less," I said, my hair standing straight up in the air. Candice laughed when she saw me. I'd forgotten that my hair is untamable in the mornings and now I'd revealed the awful and terrible truth. I look like hell in the morning. Candice, of course, looked radiant and fresh scrubbed. Her clothes appeared unwrinkled and her clear complexion and wrinkleless face made me jealous. Oh well, I thought, time will take her in the end; time compels all men.

The sun was bright, crisp, and hot across the early dew. Candice handed me a cup of steaming coffee and I drank it judiciously as it tasted like hell. She sat across from me on the table and smiled as I swilled the putrid beverage. "Good coffee sweetie. I love to wake up to the smell of a fresh pot of coffee." I lied, and felt no remorse for my lie. I'd lied to save the feelings of a truly wonderful girl. If I am doomed to hell for this, I will have words with God.

"I made it just for you," Candice said as I nodded and smiled in return. It is just such an exchange that angers me about the world. How it is that we criticize and ridicule and demoralize all the good intentions of people. As if beauty were only truly beautiful if it passes our inspection. A poem can be beautiful and pale in comparison to Shakespeare; a novel can refresh the soul and yet shrink under comparison to Tolstoy. So what. Why do we concern ourselves with this nonsense? It is like I said, there are no ugly waterfalls. Yes, and no ugly acts if they are born of love.

Candice pulled several bags from my van and set eggs, bacon and bread on the picnic table. A frying pan materialized and soon the smell of fresh fat and scrambled eggs wafted through the chilly morning air. I removed my sleeping bag from the tent and started folding it into a bundle. This was the first reminder to Candice that this was our last day together. I watched as a few tears ran down her soft cheeks. She wiped them away without saying a word. She was being Stoic. I packed the old canvas tent into the van and pressed my belongings around it into a square compact space. Candice set a plate on the table and loaded it with the hot food she had made. I sat and ate with unremitting hunger. The food was awful however. I wanted to gag, to spit the vile aggregate onto the undeserving ground, but I couldn't. The food had been made out of love and for that I was willing to suffer. Candice hovered over me to examine whether I was enjoying the experience. "Are the eggs the way you like them?" She asked.

"Perfect. I love these eggs."

"I'll make some more."

"Oh. No thanks sweetie. I like to travel light. Have a four hour drive ahead."

"So when are you leaving?"

"I have to leave after breakfast sweetie. I'll drop you off at the lodge."

"Okay. That'll be okay." Tears started streaming down her face again and I jumped up and held her by my chest.

"Look sweetie. We knew this would end. I have a life back in the valley and you have a life back in New York."

"No, I don't. I don't have a life back in New York. I don't have a life anywhere."

"What do you mean? You have law school. You'll meet some Ivy League type and fall in love and have a great life."

"No Allen. I won't. I have cancer. This is my last trip, anywhere."

I sat on the bench, stunned, my legs rubbery and cold. A thousand thoughts jammed my head and I couldn't speak for minutes. Finally, I rubbed my chin and blurted.

"I love you Candice. I mean it. You are the most special girl." Candice cried into my chest for half an hour as I stroked her hair and wiped her face. "How long? Have you been told?"

"Three, maybe four months."

"Are they sure?"

"Sure. It's inoperable. I just want to make it to Christmas. I want another Christmas with my family."

"You'll have it sweetie. I'm sure of it." I sat and pondered the meaning of my association with this girl from nowhere. I'd met her two days before in circumstances that filled the world with a blistering light. The world through her eyes had seemed magical, mysterious and wonderful. Now life seemed the harsh brute I know it to be. Behind the soft light of dawn and the orange hues of the summer sunset the terrible ill-clothed tyrant death had been lurking all along.

"If there is a heaven sweetie, you will go there."

"Do you think so Allen? Really?"

"Whatever lies beyond the door of death is more than we have ever been able to imagine. Worlds without end. Eternities beyond human understanding. This little life is a game, a flawed game that robs the poor and enriches the wealthy. Some are born with less than a full package of light. Some are born of anger and steal the light of others. On the world spins, playing the game. Only life never declares a winner. In the end we all must lose our battle to stay on the dancing orb. The point of life is to teach us the rules by which eternity is played. Then we graduate to a new existence, a new realm. This dream of earth is only a shadow, cast from the teachers who teach the souls of men. It is their only hope that we will one day be just like them."

"I hope you're right my love. I'll find out soon enough. Let's get you packed and on your way. I have to call my folks in New York in an hour. They wouldn't approve of us you know."

"No one approves of joy, unless they've first stamped it with their bile."

"Come now, that's a little harsh. My folks think anyone over twenty five is too old for me."

"Sorry, got carried away. Let's get this mess inside the van. I need to go. Tomorrow is a work day."

"Okay cowboy, let's pack stack and hit the rack."

"That makes no sense," I laughed, and it was a beautiful laugh that broke the spell of death.

"Shut up," she said as she tossed a folded camping chair into my chest.

We finished loading the van and there was nothing left to do but hop in and ramble down the road to the lodge. It was a quiet trip. Neither of us spoke more than one or two words. My heart sank with the passing of every minute. I pulled into the lodge parking lot and rested the clunker near the front entrance. I hopped out and lifted Candice from the seat. She seemed slight and delicate as if made of balsa wood. She stood by the door and looked at me, struggling to memorize every line of my being. I looked past her toward the blue lake. Squirrels scattered and birds hovered as I waited to find the right words, but they never came. I stood as a deaf mute looking out across the deep water. Candice kissed me hard on the lips.

"Give me your address so I can send you a Christmas card." I pulled a slip of paper out of the glove box and wrote the numbers on the front as my own tears made little streaks across the blue lines. I handed her the paper, which she tucked into her shirt pocket, then she turned and entered the lodge. All the light of the world vanished with her and I stood in a room of darkness that encircled the whole of creation.

I walked over to the edge of the lake and thought for a moment of diving in. How sweet would be the stillness of death, I thought. But in the end I knew myself to be a survivor, a hanger-on, and a clinger to life at all costs. I fired up the van and stuttered onto the highway encircling the lake. I'd looked forward to this drive since first spying the road on Friday, but now it seemed like a long, black ribbon to nowhere. I drove slow, aching to remember Candice's face and praying she would live to see Christmas. It seemed the least God could do. I watched a bald eagle soar over the caldera and stopped at a lookout to ogle the great bird as it soared and landed. Despite the pain, I thought, there is a glorious beauty to the world. I re-entered the van and drove on.

At last I reached the turnoff to the Willamette Valley. I made my peace with Crater Lake, with Candice and with life. It was all out of my hands anyway. I had no say in the course of the world. I wasn't the one responsible for the sorrow. I was only a man. A man who had met a beautiful lake, a beautiful woman, and had experienced a beautiful moment that would, over time, melt into a memory sweeter than the taste of summer sun on white flesh. As I drove I wondered where the next few years might take me. I had no idea, perhaps to marriage again, or to writing a book. For the first time in my life I was happy I possessed a tomorrow. I slipped into my driveway and found everything just as I'd left it. Except me.

In December of that year I received a Christmas card from New York. Inside was a picture of a bright young girl tossing snowballs at a woman. It was Candice and her mother. Candice looked happy, contented. I sent one back to her, but it was returned unopened. A month later I received a funeral notice with a crisp note from Candice's mother saying Candice had spoken often of this wonderful man she had met at Crater Lake. That she had found this address in Candice's things and hoped I was the party to which she had referred. She wished me well and said that her daughter had died peacefully in her sleep. Twenty-three is too young to die, I thought. None of us ever get the time to live as we wish. The world simply swallows us and spits our carcass into the great wall of time. The only thing we have that makes us human is the ability to dream and the courage to die before our time.

19

Death is only a failure of the condemned to meet the criteria of survival, but the tenacity, the hunger, the drive to live is absolute. Even the suicide wills to live, only in a better world. Along the vast patches of wind driven sand dunes edging the Oregon coast near Florence I stopped one day to walk out in the islands of trees that sit among the dunes like oasis's in a sea of grains. It was January and a fresh, hard-bitten storm had just pummeled the shore. A strong, cutting wind blew as I parked in a vacant parking lot next to Cleawox Lake. The sand-filled air punished my face as I walked into it toward the ocean and all about me was the deafening silence of emptiness.

I hiked first up to the tip of the highest dune. From that peak it is possible to run down the full length of the face and dive headfirst into the lake. Beyond the peak the ocean lies more than a mile away. The Pacific is sheltered by a berm of sand covered by grass. Inside of this berm lies what is called a deflation plain, where the ground is actually equal to sea level. In between these two points, the peak and the berm, lay acres of sand piled in bumpy mounds. Here and there a few islands of trees and brush have formed where the sand has failed to completely capture the forest that once inhabited this area. The islands are vaulted expanses that fill the eye with mystery. I faced into the biting wind, bundled my hood around my head and marched toward an island of trees to the southeast.

As I walked my feet sank into the soft, dry sand making each step a physical challenge. The cold air rushed past my face and made my eyes water to the point of invisibility. I could only see the tips of the tallest trees so I headed for them though this path included too many ups and downs. I listened to the wind as it spoke. I heard the whips and whistles of sand grains carried aloft by the air, the wind filling my ears with alternating pitches and silences.

I reached the first island in a half hour and walked to the top via a well-worn trail. Sheltered by the trees the wind could not reach my face and I lowered my hood to allow the salty ocean air to penetrate. At the top I discovered a bench made of old logs and broken branches. I sat and stared toward the ocean enjoying the utter silence of the human species. I could hear no cars, no trucks, and no machinery. I heard no weeping or wailing or screams of pain. I heard no desperation or tales of conquest. I heard only the sea, the wind, and the bending of trees. I sat for a long time, uncertain if I wanted to stay, leave or travel onward. I'd never walked to the ocean from the sand dunes because it is a perilous journey and a stickery brush that makes passage all but impossible guards the ocean. However, from my perch I saw one possible avenue to the sea. I memorized the hills and valleys to the area and marched down the island and out across the desert of dunes toward the sea.

A half hour later blisters formed on the soles of my feet and the lack of water formed crusty realms on my lips. But as I looked toward the ocean it still looked far away. I was isolated and alone and the silence was comforting, but the knowledge that I'd committed to a long, arduous journey made me feel like a fool. The wind whipped my face harder as the slow gusts gave way to vibrant gushers of air. The grains of sand in the wind cut my face like thousands of tiny razors. I lowered my head, pulled my coat as tight around me as possible and walked with great effort toward the sea.

I don't know when it happened or why, but I began to dream, though I was awake. The absence of human contact and human noise had placed me in another world; a world made of both real and imagined objects. I heard birds that were not there and watched animals dart across the sand that do not live near the ocean. This is why I cannot verify as real what I'm about to tell you. If this vision was only a fiction concocted in my head, then the scene is still of value, and if it was indeed real, then the world is a very mysterious place. I reached the sea via the narrow path through the thickets and found myself in a depression between two small mounds of sand. That is when I saw it.

Sitting in the valley where the full force of the wind would beat on it every day a delicate purple violet grew. It was not perfect and round, as one would be in my garden, but it had the shape and color of a violet, though I have never heard of violets growing on the coast. But the little flower had thrived in an area that prohibited life in almost any form. I couldn't see anything else living within a hundred feet of my body. The flowers color and richness startled me. I rubbed my eyes, but there it still was, proud and resolute, unwilling to conceded its life to the hounding wind.

I looked across the gray-blue water and sensed a coming storm. I wondered if the flower would survive, but then I realized this flower must have already weathered hundreds of storms. I watched a seagull loft overhead and land by the water. I watched a fishing vessel out to sea and wondered if the violet had any awareness of how perilous a life it was living. Then I realized that no man or plant or animal truly understands the position they play in life. All living things are only momentary openings in a closing sea of time. I do not sit and constantly contemplate the end of my life. So too the little violet at my feet was living its tiny life, unaware of the dangerous and certain tides that must ultimately seal its fate.

I lowered my head again as the wind bit ever harder. The violet bent and swayed in the harsh breeze, but it remained anchored in the sand. I watched until I could stand up no more. I plopped onto the sand and wanted to pluck the little flower and take it back to show everyone what a treasure I'd found in the dunes. But as I listened to the wind and tasted the salt of the sea on my lips I could not bring myself to pluck the victorious creature. What right did I have to end the struggling of another living thing that had worked so hard just to survive? There was nobility in the struggle, power in the strife, beauty in the color of violet edged against the plain auburn sand. In the end I walked away.

I hiked to my car and shook off the sand from my coat, my face, and my shoes. I wished for a moment that I'd carried the flower back with me, to be able to smell it on the way home and be reminded of the coming spring, the season I love. But I knew I'd done the honorable thing. I wondered if this was indeed the struggle of God, to desire to pluck a man from his suffering before his time, though he has made his life noble by the constant resistance to his ultimate death. I think I will ask God one day, if I see Him. I've searched many times for other violets in the dunes, but have never found any. The violet was one of a kind, as are all things that have ever lived on earth. If we can claim only one victory over our brief lives, it is this unalterable fact.

20

Most of the country thinks of Oregon as a land of green valleys and oceans, waterfalls and trees, but in truth Oregon is a land of mountains and volcanic residue. The majority of the state lies to the east of the Cascade Mountains and is filled with lava, cinder cones, barren wastes and harsh terrain. Near Bend the two worlds collide in a kaleidoscope of diversity. From Bend one can see the austere Cascades and the volcanic residue that has filled the basin of central Oregon with a special beauty. The land of central Oregon is as diverse as the human race. One moment a grove of trees, the next a flourishing river, the next a cinder cone that reminds us that the world was created on the back of molten rock. They call central Oregon a wonderland and it is. While I was a student at Oregon State University I took a weekend class to the area where I explored the terrain and the lava tubes.

I signed up to take a field trip to central Oregon during my senior year at Oregon State. I needed one credit to graduate on time and the weekend class offered a grand opportunity not only to fulfill my graduation requirements but also to explore areas I had never been to. I packed light and greeted the bus by Gill Coliseum, full of enthusiasm and a hunger for adventure. I waited for some time until at last several other travelers assembled by the old building and awaited their trip to the unknown. By the time the instructor arrived a rag tag troop of campers and hikers had assembled with varying arrays of gear. Some sported backpacks, others small tents and coolers. I couldn't see how all of it would fit into the narrow bus, but I was astonished a half hour later when the last piece of equipment had been carefully loaded aboard.

I looked for people of common stock, people who might be willing to share a laugh or to howl at the moon. Some students looked too serious and others looked too unfettered by reality. Finally, I caught a glimpse of two girls that stood out from the pack. They were laughing and giggling. Ordinarily I like to keep to myself but this one weekend I was in a mood to socialize and get to know new people. I was sick of school, sick of rain and needed a diversion from the humdrums of my daily life. I picked the seat directly behind the two girls and was happy when no one took the seat to my side.

The bus ride to Bend was long, arduous and dull. The scenery crossing over the Cascades was spectacular but the entire bus of strangers made little more than a few grunts as the hours past. Even the silly girls to my front fell asleep on route. I watched out my window as the tree lines changed from Douglas Fir to Ponderosa Pine, as the green shafts of land turned to brown and reddish purple and the heat of the valley turned into blistering waves of searing pain as we crossed into the east. Even the valiant air conditioner could not keep the heat from burning my face. I sat and awaited our arrival into camp.

We at last came into Bend, a flourishing city formed from the outcasts of California, Oregon retirees, and the adventurous. From Bend it is possible to ski the grand slopes of Mount Bachelor where skiing is year around. It is possible to raft the Deshutes River, to horseback ride or to do, as we were about to risk, climb into caves made from balls of gas that formed when the area was molten and unformed. It is a land of limitless possibilities and has grown from a sleepy village of 12,000 in the sixties to a thriving mini-metropolis of over 50,000. The sun shines more than 300 days a year in Bend and all we valley dwellers can do is point to the lush green of our wet world, while the central Oregonians wear their t-shirts and tennis shorts on their way out of doors.

I was disappointed when we left the secure confines of Bend and headed out of town due north on a little used highway which became a rough road, then a gravel road, then a dirt road, then no road at all. The campground into which we had reserved several sites turned out to be a "primitive" site, which meant a fire pit and a pull off. I was not the only one groaning at the site. I had hoped for pools, hiking trails, mountain biking, and sunbathing. What was in store was no showers, no water, no firewood and no fun. I unloaded my gear and pitched my small tent next to the two girls who were yet to understand that I'd selected them as my temporary friends.

The girls, nice wholesome types, neither pretty or plain, reached a snag in their set up and came over to ask for assistance, which I readily supplied. "Hi, I'm Heidi and this is Sarah. We can't seem to get our tent up right. Could you possibly give us a hand?"

"Sure thing. My name's Allen by the way. Let's take a look." I walked over to their tent and realized these two co-eds were unprepared for the days ahead. They had set their tent up right over a bevy of tiny boulders that would make for harsh sleeping. Then they had placed the tent so their heads would be pointing downhill. I just scrapped all of their efforts and started anew. When I'd finished they looked at me with utter respect and astonishment and our friendship was formed.

"Thank you so much Allen," Sarah said. Sarah was a tall, thin redhead with a clear complexion. I guessed her age to be about twenty-one, eight years my junior, and she spoke with the crispness of someone tutored all her life by over anxious English teacher parents. However, this formality was counter pointed by a direct goofiness, which I found from the outset to be deliciously fun. Heidi was a dark-haired heavyset girl, though not fat, and she had a laugh that could fill a chamber of magma with reverberating madness. I liked them both instantly and I did not know why, but sometimes it is our subconscious that does our choosing for us, thank God. I tend toward people who look as if they are lost in a wilderness, but not necessarily wanting to get out of the woods. The majority of people hold no more interest to me than a pile of rocks.

The instructor, a forty-something bearded professor of God knew what, had us meet in the middle of the camp for lunch. Afterwards we loaded back into the bus for our first adventure, spelunking the Lava River Cave that ultimately would have us about two hundred feet under the earth. I climbed aboard and sat behind the two girls again, who were eager and flushed with excitement about getting to go down into a real cave. I was more skeptical, but nonetheless excited. The bus pulled out and we landed in the parking lot an hour later. There were cars from every state in the union in the lot and I wondered just how unique our experience was going to be.

The entire group, twenty-five souls in all, marched up to a brown shack at the trailhead and our instructor informed us we would each need a lantern or a strong flashlight, as there was no lighting in the cave. I rented a lantern, which glowed brightly if not steadily, and the girls opted for flashlights in need of new batteries. The troop entered the cave and quickly the outrageous heat of the day evaporated into a musky coolness that froze the sweat on my legs and sent a chill up my spine. I was wishing I'd brought a jacket, but wishing did not make one appear out of the musty air.

I fell in behind the majority, watching in fascination as they disappeared into the black chamber. The girls lagged behind until they formed at either side of me due to the dimness of their flashlights. I walked straight and sure through the initial tunnel until the walls receded and gave way to a large, thunderous cavern with walls more than fifty feet wide. Here we caught up with the instructor who was spewing forth the history of our planet from the beginning of time. I could not have been less interested. What I was interested in was the adventure, so the three of us marched along oblivious to the discussion echoing around us.

The girls were getting cold and so each of them took an arm and gripped for dear life as I was the only light among the shadows. As we walked occasional dips and stairs led us further into the depths. The cold and the tightness of the tube made for shutters and shakes. Lava tubes are formed when gas bubbles form within flowing lava and then after the lava hardens the gas escapes and leaves a funnel in which to spend a weekend. There are hundreds if not thousands of these tubes in eastern Oregon, some so remote there are no roads to them. Before long the three of us had left all others behind and the relief of the occasional room was followed by the sheer terror of the tightness of the next section of tube. We grinned and struggled until at last we found ourselves crawling on hands and knees.

Sarah was having a grand time, but Heidi was not. A minor case of claustrophobia was causing her forehead to shed drops of sweat. The chamber narrowed even more and slight panic crept into my heart. I'd never been fond of dark, tight spaces, having crawled under numerous houses in my time, but the fact of being over a hundred feet below the surface placed stress on my courage. Fortunately, I was the legal guardian of two young women so to play the part of the strong, fearless man I hid my concerns amid deep, gasping breaths. Sarah was behind me during the crawl and goosed me twice, which caused the lantern to nearly blow out. I chastised her but secretly liked the attention. Sarah appeared to have no concern whatsoever for the reality of life. To her it was all fun and games. At the time I thought her immature, but now in the throes of middle age I miss her laugh. I hope the man who married her loves her dearly and has not killed her laugh.

We reached the end of the tube after much crawling and wiggling. The end was a bit of a disappointment as it was only a small area that allowed four or five people to sit cross-legged. The three of us sat and thought about where we were at that moment, deep under the earth in a tiny cavern with no light and no escape if an earthquake should happen that instant. "Do you think we should turn out the light and see what it's like in total darkness," Sarah asked. Heidi looked concerned, but adventurous.

"Sure, why not. Let's get the crap scared out of us," Heidi replied. I turned down the lantern until blackness enveloped us. Sarah and Heidi started to sing a song from kid's camp I had not heard in twenty years, something about pirates and boats. I sang along as the trio of our voices echoed out of the chamber and caught the coming pilgrims unawares.

We continued for several minutes until new recruits arrived and joined in the singing. The vibrations from our singing rang down our spines and into our tingling feet. Then I realized our light had gone out, forever. So had the light of our new comrades. We had to touch each other to find the way out and Sarah did not flinch when my hand glided across her breasts. I pushed her out of the exit and one by one we followed, occasionally touching the back of each other until we emerged from the narrow neck of the tunnel and late comers supplied us with a refill of light. We continued out of the tunnel until we emerged into the heat of the late afternoon. I was blinded for several minutes until I could finally make out the faces of Heidi and Sarah. Heidi's face was covered in black as she had applied mascara earlier in the day and it had melted under the rivers of shedding sweat. Sarah and I laughed at Heidi so she wiped some of the residue on our shirts.

We languished in the heat or almost an hour before all of the other trekkers had exited the cave. The instructor came out an announced that he had failed to go all the way and wanted to know if anyone had. The three of us raised our hands. He asked what it was like and Sarah responded. "It was small, dark and scary."

"Well," the instructor said, "That cave was much wider than the one we'll conquer tomorrow." I cringed. Sarah and Heidi looked at each other and smiled. The travelers loaded onto the awaiting bus and we made it back to camp about suppertime. The instructor built a huge fire, which all of us used to cook on and the group at last got around to introductions and personal backgrounds and the tightness of the early day gave way to familiarity and frivolity. Sarah kept the group in stitches with her impressions of well-known Oregon State professors.

That night Sarah convinced me to leave my tent and sleep with her and Heidi under the stars. I resisted, but was soon glad I'd accepted the invitation. The stars were thick that night and the clarity of the dark, high desert sky is haunting. Sarah laughed until one in the morning as Heidi and I humored her until we fell asleep. I doubt if Sarah slept more than two hours, but in the morning she was fresher and more ready than all of us. I was amazed by her tenacity and capacity for adventure. Sarah teased me in the morning that she had secretly raped me in the night and that she was now pregnant. I processed multitudes of unpleasant feelings of fatherhood before allowing it to be a joke. I told her I was sterile so it must have been the instructor, an ugly, strangely configured man. She said, "Ewwwww." I promised her that the child would look like him, but be a girl. She tickled me and laughed. Heidi for some reason looked jealous.

After an uneventful breakfast we loaded onto the bus and started a tour of the back roads of eastern Oregon. We left pavement after only five miles and journeyed to the north into the flat, barren wastelands covered in fields of loose lava. The instructor kept pointing to lava tubes we were passing by but all we could see was the occasional hole in the ground. These were not tourist centers by any means, but out of the way adventure for the curious. Sarah and Heidi played a game that involved the slapping of alternate hands as I watched the desert for signs of life.

The bus slowed and we settled near a narrow hole less than five feet from the road, which was no more than a rutted path in the desert. We off loaded and stood surrounding the hole, astonished that we were about to enter this cave in the middle of nowhere. I was uncertain, at that point, if the instructor knew the way back to camp. Even the mountains were little help as they surrounded us on all sides. The instructor led a small group of six students into the hole and asked all of us to join in three at a time so as not to clog the opening which was narrower than most. We obliged and Sarah, Heidi and I waited until the end and I leapt down the hole first. I was startled by what I found.

Beyond the tiny opening a great room spread out until it seemed that the whole of the world was nothing more than a thin veneer over an underworld of caves. Heidi and Sarah climbed down after me and the three of us stared at the immensity of the cave with disbelieving eyes. The instructor was hotly engaged in a discussion of magma chambers and gas bubbles, which bored me to tears so the three of us set out along the east wall to a channel that narrowed to nothingness. Two other hardy souls followed, but turned back when the chamber looked impassible except as a belly crawl. I looked at the tiny passageway and thought for a moment then offered an opinion. "I say let's do it. What the hell, they can't leave us here. They have to rescue us if we get lost." Sarah looked up to the challenge, but Heidi's face cast a pale shadow on the thick wall. "Oh come on Heidi, live a little. Who knows what's beyond this passage, maybe buried treasure." With that the two school girls, pigtails and all, laughed for several minutes.

I took the first leap of faith. I crouched into a half ball and walked about a hundred feet until the ceiling lowered beyond my ability to hunch. I lay out on my stomach as the ceiling narrowed to a pinch. Heidi followed me, but Sarah did not. I was surprised. As I crawled, the floor became moist and my shirt soaked through with seepage from the cave. "Ewwww," Heidi said, her favorite word, "This is sick." I crawled onward struggling harder for breath as the passage became only big enough for large rats and small men. Heidi followed me like a pilgrim to Mecca. A hundred feet further down the chamber we ran into a slight difficulty. The floor of the chamber, once only a wet weeping mess, had turned into a thousand pin prick points jabbing me in ways unimaginable and in unimaginable places. I winced in pain and Heidi threw a tantrum. "Damn you Allen, what did you get us into here? What if we can't go on and we can't back up?"

"Then we'll die here and some school boy of the twenty-first century will find our rodent picked bones," I said. She slapped my foot with her available hand and it stung like hell.

About fifty feet further, after the pain had subsided into only a dull ache, the ceiling began to expand and the little chamber opened into a room filled with wonders beyond anything we had yet seen. Stalagmites and stalactites hung up and down, weeping walls covered in colors of the rainbow and rock formations that possessed the shapes of horse heads, men, birds and creatures of the night. It was wondrous. "Wow, look at this it's unbelievable," Heidi said, "To think that all this lay past all that pain."

"Kind of like man's hope of eternal life," I offered.

"Yea, exactly, yea, I like that. Cool thinking Allen." Just then a voice echoed through the chamber. It was Sarah.

"Guys, guys, are you in here? I'm scared, say something, anything."

I couldn't resist. I huddled up to the opening and bellowed low, ominous tones into the hole. "Ohhhhhmmmm. Ahhhhhhmmmmm. HOOOOOhhhoooooo."

"Stop it. Stop it right now Allen. I know that's you," Sarah said in a half believable voice.

"Nooooooo. I ate him and that girl. YUMMmmmmmm." I heard hard crawling as water splished and points pricked. Strange guttural noises emanated from the tube until at last a red head appeared at the opening. I got on my hands and knees and came up to Sarah's head. "Chomp, chomp." A hand reached up and grabbed my nose and yanked hard. "Owwh."

Sarah climbed to her feet. "Let's get him." The two girlish forms attacked front and rear and I was soon on the ground staring up at the Sistine Chapel of nature. "Tickle him. Hard." I felt long fingernails dig into my sides and one set of fingers pinched my butt until it hurt. I rolled over to try and escape and the two of them pinned me with their weight to the floor. "Got you now. What are you going to do about it?" Sarah giggled. I was helpless underneath them, but laughing too hard to gain control of my superior strength. I decided to pinch back. My counterattack worked as one of my pinchers found Heidi's nipple and she whelped in agony and rolled off. I turned over and grabbed Sarah, all one hundred and five pounds of her, and lifted her up as my legs found the floor. I squeezed her hard and she squeezed back. "I'm not letting go," Sarah shouted, so loud the echo could be heard reverberating a dozen times across the room.

We stood in the middle of the room hands clenched and bodies interwoven as Heidi looked on in quiet disbelief. I hugged Sarah harder and began to jostle her up and down as she let out a soft uggghhhhhh. The sound was ridiculous and all three of us burst into uncontrollable laughter. I fell to the ground and Heidi and Sarah fell on top of me and we joined in a group hug that seemed made of more genuine affection than any before or since. "You girls are the best," I said at last.

"You too Allen. You're way too much fun. And to think Heidi thought you were a stuffed shirt when we first saw you."

"Stuffed shirt!" I railed.

"Yep," Heidi stated, "Very stuffed." She landed a soft fist into my belly and I got the pun. We lay on the weeping floor for several minutes, our arms all intermingled, and made ridiculous uhghhhs and aghhhhs just to hear the silly sounds echo back to us as we lay together.

After awhile a very angry instructor could be heard through the tunnel threatening to leave us here if we didn't come out immediately. Reluctantly, we filed into the tube for the treacherous journey back. As we emerged from the tunnel the entire class was standing around with a bizarre look plastered on their faces. They had thought we were lost. The three of us stood together and offered up a lame excuse for our behavior. "I thought it was another way out," I said. The instructor, at last too curious for further admonishment, asked.

"Just what's in there anyway?"

"Lost treasure."

We spent the rest of the day traveling in and out of several more tubes but none of them matched the glory of the secret hole we three had found. Toward early evening we straggled back to camp and I fell exhausted onto my sleeping bag. Heidi cooked my supper for me and brought it to me in a big blackened pot. I thank her profusely and she wiped a hand across my forehead and said, "We're friends now."

In the morning we reloaded the bus and headed to Bend to take in the High Desert Museum and to ride the perilous trolley to the top of a cinder cone. Heidi, Sarah and I held hands all day which brought repeated stares, but we didn't care, we were locked into our own world and to tell the truth it was a damn sight better than this one. On the ride to the cinder cone Sarah started singing her boat song again and this time the entire bus got into the act and we sounded like a gang of grade-school kids at a YMCA camp. I loved it. I'd spent four years, almost, in college and had lost my ability to enjoy the simple pleasures of life. Sarah and Heidi had reengaged my sense of fun and I was wallowing in the grand gloriousness of it. They, however, were only being their every day selves. I admired them more than words can tell.

At five o'clock sharp we arrived back at Gill Coliseum. The bus was quickly off loaded and I stood beside my stack of gear and waited to say good-bye to the two girls. They had made my trip so enjoyable. Sarah and Heidi ran up to me and hugged me hard. "Goodbye Allen. Thanks for the wonderful time."

"I should thank you two."

"Why?" Heidi asked.

"Because you reminded me what fun life is supposed to be."

"That's the way we were both raised my friend. Someone did you wrong."

"The world did me wrong."

I had a terrible time letting go of them. I did not want to go back to the world from which I had sprung. I wanted to live in their world, to live with them in the simple pleasure of a summer day, but the world beckoned me back. I have never been pleased with the world since. I looked many times about campus for the two girls, but I never saw them again. I graduated soon after and entered the real world of work and worry. I have never stopped looking for these two friends. I seek them in stores and in classes, in work and in playgrounds, but they are no more. When I look back across some of the chapters of this book I realize that many of my subsequent encounters with women, while engaged in the natural world, have been my feeble attempts to rekindle what I found, and lost, in the lava tubes of Bend. I carry the memory of Sarah and Heidi deep within my heart. I cherish them. If Sarah and Heidi ran the world, I've always believed, we all might wish to live forever.

21

The Columbia River gorge, running between the states of Oregon and Washington, was once a raging inferno of water. The first pioneers took great pains to avoid its treacherous falls and swirls by crossing over the Cascade Mountains. But now a series of dams have turned the once turbulent river into a calm and placid expanse. Through myriads of centuries a channel has been cut by the river until now the basin looks like a valley carved by a separation of the earth. For centuries Native Americans have fished these waters for salmon. Now most of the fish are gone. However, the scenery remains.

In the 1920's a great road-building project commenced along the banks of the Columbia. The result was a spectacular, if narrow, roadway through a canyon of water that passes along the bottom pools of several waterfalls. I've taken this trip many times, but it never grows tiresome. From the Vista Overlook to the replica of Stonehenge the basin commands a deep, abiding respect from all its travelers. The views presented are worth every effort to veer off the interstate and ride through the twists and turns of old highway 30. The ancient rock bridges and the berms of boulders, Multnomah Lodge and the Vista Overlook are the brave remains of this early twentieth century vision. I defy anyone to cross into this land and not be amazed at how blest a land Oregon truly is. I've never met the equal of this land of rain. Through the rains of winter comes the bounty of spring, the green trees and grass, the wildlife, the deer and elk, the salmon and the coho, the steelhead and the trout. And all this grandeur lorded over by the old mountain, Mt. Hood.

One summer day I drove onto highway 30 and stopped at Multnomah Lodge to hike up to the top of Multnomah Falls, the highest in the state of Oregon. Across the pool at the bottom a bridge spans the trickling creek and I stood for several minutes on the span to snap pictures. I watched as several hearty souls ventured back from the trail to the top and noticed copious beads of sweat glistening on their bodies. I walked across the bridge to the trailhead and discovered the trail wound straight up for over a hundred feet via a switchback system. I mustered my determination to climb to the top and began my journey by placing one foot in front of the other. I huffed, puffed, sweated, nearly fainted and almost cried, but I succeeded in climbing to the edge of a waterfall considered among the most beautiful in the world.

At the drop off point a small wooden alcove had been built to allow one to stand out over the water and watch the water drop to the pool below. It is the only time in my life I've ever understood the full power of falling water. I watched the untamed water tumble and attempted to trace the destiny of a single drop, but the multitudes of competitors made the journey impossible to track. I looked across the Columbia Basin and watched small vessels navigate the river and then watched travelers as they snapped pictures from the bridge beneath. How sad, I thought, that they do not venture up to this height. It is a magical place. It is the one place in Oregon where serenity can be achieved in the presence of others.

I descended then followed the old highway to its conclusion, basking in the lush growth of trees. I turned right at the end and headed south toward Mount Hood. The back country of rural Oregon is not as green as the Willamette Valley, but it is just as alluring. The rocky outcrops, the creeks and rivers, the shrubbery and the working ranches all lend a vital eminence to the land. I made a final right turn and pulled my car up a steep road toward the parking lot at Timberline Lodge, a grand reminder of the depression and the government's attempts to put people back to work. The lot is approximately the altitude of Crater Lake and areas of the Mount Jefferson Wilderness. I'd journeyed full circle.

I lunged into an open parking space and set my emergency brake full force because the lot sloped downward to a bottom I cared not to find. I stood beside the old lodge and admired the wooden textures, the old world style, and the rough exterior of the grand beast. Timberline Lodge was built during the depression and was dedicated by President Franklin Roosevelt himself. The work employed the skills of hundreds of craftsmen and artisans. The old lodge is stuffed with the charm of a bygone era, an era when buildings and furnishings were made to last multiple lifetimes. And now in it's 70's the old lodge has proven the wisdom of that thinking. I walked over to a series of concrete steps and entered the lodge. I came first to a grand fireplace surrounded by some of the original chairs. I walked through the chambers and rooms and felt a sense of longing for the world from which the old lodge had sprung.

I walked out onto the back patio and gazed up at the peak of Mount Hood. I noticed a chairlift still running though it was the dead of August. I raced over to the lift shack and bought a ticket for the ride up. I was placed in a chair as a metal bar came down over the top of me to act as my only security from falling to my death. The lift seemed much higher without the ten feet of snow that is underneath it in winter. I arrived at the top of the ski slope, hopped off and stumbled. I laughed the whole scene off as misguided enthusiasm. I ambled to a series of rocks and sat on the largest of the three and stared across the expanse of the Cascade Mountains and the Willamette Valley, which lies at the mountain's feet. I could see all of Oregon, or so it seemed, and the richness of the land settled into me and I understood at last that I'd been born into privilege under a canopy of rain, a rain that blankets my world.

I sat on the top of the mountain gazing from Portland to the plateaus of the east until the day came quietly to an end. The sun sank beyond the ridges of the Coast Range Mountains as orange and pink light etched its way across the entirety of the sky. I carved the moment into my mind, into my memories, so that if I was ever pulled away from this glorious womb I'd be able to dust off my primeval memories and live again in the valley of the true life. I drove home and fell asleep in my bed uncertain which of my two worlds was most real, mountain or hearth. I dreamed of my valley and understood for the first time the meaning of the rain. It is not the mountains or the trees or the babbling brooks that make a paradise, it is the flow of what lies between them.

THE RAIN POEMS

A FLOWER BLOOMS

What is time that it stops for you,
Like a seed it cannot keep?
Oh to sleep, sleep, sleep,
Then to bloom like a spring fresh flower
In the meadow, wild and meek.

TO THE SEA

Bathe me in a beauty deep,
Upon the memories that I keep,
As I walk to the salty brine,
This journey is a thought of mine,
To see the shadow of the sea,
To build a bridge to eternity.

Oh the sea is calling me,
Beyond the barriers of the dock,
Like a sick and slow false clock,
I must venture to the setting sun,
Until my work is drowned in days,
One by one by one.

TOWARD AN UNKNOWN SUN

A star that shines so near to earth,
It is a yellow sphere of birth,
A torrid thought of gifts through years,
A searing cue of risks and odds,
A guardian of eternal light,
A ball that tapers into night,
It polishes the secrets of summer days,
Of men, and gods, and deeper ways,
I will look to daylight's prayer,
And find sweet heaven weeping there.

I CHASED A FLOWING RIVER

Under the bridge that crosses into town,
I tried to chase a rambling river down,
But in my haste I could not seem to bear,
That when I came there was no river there.

OF TIME AND THE REDWOOD TREE

What is this, of which I hear in vain,
That time is sealed in trees that hide the rain,
I hear of tales that seeds have grown to gods,
And sprouted to the sky against the odds?

The soil rich and lavish in its praise,
Has these mighty trees been its to raise,
And in this vaunted task that time has sown,
A thousand gifts of light have this earth grown.

I stand and gawk at trees that touch the clouds,
And think that bristling birds are all so loud,
But it is in the quick and reverent schemes,
That nature hides its choicest ruling themes.

So if I hear the gentle giants wake,
It will be my hour to beauty slake,
And see the aching of time we have not bred,
And hear the whispered silence of the dead.

CEMETERY DAY

I stride amid the markers high and low,
And see the years in numbers that I know,
The graves are old and tattered to the ground,
I think upon the names that I have found.
So long the grass has roofed this rumbled yard,
That houses souls and dreams and tears,
So many of the town lay here,
Drifted through the days and years.
I knew them once, or some at least,
Now they are asleep, at peace,
I drift among the avenues,
Of marble, dirt, cement and sod,
It is the street of life's retreat,
A step to life with God.
I listen to the ravens caw,
And robins flit on trees,
I lift a weed from near a grave,
And pluck it on my knees.
I smell the fresh cut odor of spring grass,
Mixed with air and earth and ash,
I walk among the rows and rows,
That mark the path where heaven goes.
I think of trials that these that lie here knew,
And wonder if their troubles lie here too,
And if I might one day a respite find,
Among the kindred markers of mankind.

INTO THIS LIFE

Into this life a man is thrust to die,
His mind is crammed with knowledge
And his life is fleshed in tears,
To mock him as a trifling in the spheres,
And empty out his bank account of years.

UPON A HILL THAT SINGS

The hilltop is a rounded dome,
That rises to a dusty throne,
I climb to see the fields and fodder new,
And find the twilight hiding in the dew.

Down the hill I fall to reach the lane,
And feel a sharp abrasion soaked in pain,
As my body is resistant to my soul,
Who wants to live forever on this knoll.

RIGHT AS RAIN

Out a window streaked in rain,
I see the fate of tears upon the pane,
And think of words that might be mine to keep,
And wish a futile promise on the sleet.

Out the window I see the slick retreat,
Of life into the moment filled with gray,
And wish a long tomorrow in the sun,
And watch the drip of water on the glass,
And slip into a memory that is past.

A pounding sun now takes this sodden sight,
And fills the window with a vagrant, brooded light,
Who among the world can see through rain,
And exit through this window without pain?

THE CITY

Awake and out the wooden door,
To glimpse the high and sheepish steel,
Of buildings that a man has made.
What is this hunger to escape
The twisted leaves of trees that dot the land,
Why from this nature have we fled,
To live among the sky
That does not breathe?
If only we could see that life
Is still, and better on the ground
Than in a dream.

AH, CLOUD

I know the answer to the riddle of the sky,
It is not a no, a not, or a why,
Clouds are homeless beggars near the sun,
They were never born and never die,
When their moisture has released,
And is vanished to the ground,
They are merely circling
Round and round.

A WALK IN RAIN

I walk under the gaze of ancient trees,
And let sweet water lap upon my tongue,
And let the dusty moisture hold my care,
And strut among the branches as I please.

HAND OUT, HOLD OUT

There is a man, who squats nearby a road,
And holds his withered hand out in the cold,
As thousands of workers pass him by,
On their way to earn their steady keep,
Caring not a wit if he should live or die.
I too pass him nimbly on my way,
Trifling through my busy, hectic day,
I never have a clever word to say,
I simply drive in shadows crammed with strife.

I want some days to give him of my bread,
That has always amply kept me fed,
But I wonder if a meal would solve his need,
Or would he be by tomorrow yet again,
Or could I make him happy with a bed.
But I drive on and so the others too,
Sometimes wondering what's a soul to do,
There are so many tired, cold, unfed,
How many can I save, or keep warm, or well,
So I drive on, sealing them forever in their hell.

A QUIET IN THE SPRING

Bold and blue the twilight new,
Dancing in the flowers that you grew,
The spring has come and freshened up
The yard,
Blooming in bright colors frozen hard.

Like the air that filters in the nose,
The sweet elixir of your rose,
Comes into the world without a trace, or clue,
That all these colored flowers came from you.

Spring skips into the world,
Year by year,
And does not understand that you're not here,
But still it brings the flowers that you kept,
Alive by all the tears that I have wept.

IN THE MEADOW

Beyond the woods I spy a sea of grass,
Filled with flowers, flying bugs and frass,
Spilled by termites chomping at a log,
Turning it to nature like a cog.

Busy fluttering in the wind,
The little armies march and spin,
In the meadow that I see,
Lives are lived by bumblebees.

A WORK IN PROGRESS

A work in progress is not done,
Not a polished product or a prize,
It is a pile of words that needs to mend,
And only time can sew up what I send,
To people that know the words
That I must write,
To be among the read and the bright,
No wonder most who start give up
The fight,
And watch long forgotten movies
Late at night.

VISIONS OF HAPPY TRUTH

Despite the evil and the lies,
Truth will ride upon our eyes,
Like lightening from the evermore,
It whirls through the open door,
Of hearts that hold a secret map to right,
Truth will ride on radiant beams of light.

TEARS

A tear falls out upon my cheek,
A drop that falls as liquid, meek,
I watch it gather to the ground,
And find its way into a creek,
That flows down toward the little stream,
A waxing, waning summer's dream,
The tiny tear drifts toward a lake,
Where there it does evaporate,
And fill the sky with puffs of white,
That lifts it toward the heaven's light.
It settles in time upon the soil,
A simple liquid tear of toil,
And finds its way to a morning new,
And settles on sod as spring sent dew,
Until I drink it wet, so sweet, so free,
And it returns again inside of me.

PRIVILEGE

Privilege is a boat upon a sea,
That rides so high and bold above the waves,
Until the wind blows hard and long,
And the boat is framed upon the tide,
And no one finds a place to hide,
From all that privilege has made to bear,
You will die in lame despair,
Because your heart was in the boat,
That could not find a way to float,
And sunk you in the depths of salt,
As all the while you claimed,
That privilege was not your fault.

SANCTUARY

When in time our time is lost to care,
Our gilded cage of worry claims us there,
Where all the days are rounded to a heap,
That in the daylight of our memory
Time will keep.

Sanctuary, take me to your door,
Let me wander in and shut out
The light of day,
Let me crawl into the dusty bin,
And wrap around your arms that gather in,
And find a brief relief from power and men,
Where I can find a collar for my crimes,
That came and washed away
Life's sovereign claim,
Upon my youthful lines,
That wrinkled in my shame.

BY THE HARBOR

I live by the harbor that men have made,
To let the boats of commerce
Rest inside,
The harbor that is safety from the tide,
That saves the brave born vessels from
The wind,
And gives a lasting savor to our cause,
Of life inside the harbor safe and free,
To venture forth is asking for a fall
From grace, which is the noblest
Harbor of them all.

I LOVED YOU

Though time has claimed it for its own,
It was once a burning, fevered thing,
That fed us in the winter, warm and wet,
Though now it is a bold and barren token,
Of all that I have done and now regret.

SPACE AND ALL THAT IN IT IS

Wide and long, the edges clear,
The halls of space, like a mirror,
Reflect the deeds of time and need,
A giant cosmic apple seed,
That grows and grows until the end,
The radiant beams of light to bend,
And into night our hearts to send,
Space and all that in it is,
Shall conquer time and place and men,
And leave a haunted shadow hung in void,
Of all that once had striven,
And had been.

I KNEW A GIRL WHO DIED

A girl, young and pleasant in her voice,
Died today, though not of conscious choice,
She hungered and clawed to live another day,
But her fragile life
Did not turn out that way,
Some are born to live longer than their peers,
Some are ripped too young from mother's tears,
But I have sure knowledge of a prayer,
That when I go to glory
I shall surely find her there.

HOW TIME DOES WEARY YOU

Life is long, yet short, yet old,
Until the beat of endless hours fail,
And men are stripped of struggle,
Their hopes and dreams to no avail.
Men seek a bastion from their role
Of soldier to the sod, to mend a moment
Under the sun, to find a solace in the wind,
But time will make you weary,
Bleed you of your vital, sacred stuff,
And leave you in the end upon a heap,
Made of promises time has failed to keep.

A WIDOW'S MITE

A widow sits rocking in her chair,
Thinking of a husband
That is not there,
She seeks the moment of his
Return, from work where he was killed
So long ago,
But on the minutes tick,
And the window is
Filled with robins nesting
In a tree,
That he planted as a seed,
He does not come though days pass on,
The world revolves, days are done,
The window empty, shaded, alone,
Though the light of love,
Through the rippled glass
Once brightly shone.

I WILL FIND A PEACE

I will not let the weeping world conspire,
To take from me the little peace I've won
Upon the battlefield of time,
Where men have died by billions,
As they worked a sovereign's crime.

I will not fret my tiny light's refrain,
From all that men on earth may
Sweat and gain,
I will freeze the moment of my stay,
In a sweetened memory as I pray,
And think of moments bathed in joy,
Before the whims of fate,
Can all my love destroy.

SUMMER

It is never too soon to see the summer sun,
The bold and vibrant eye of bluest sky,
The sun will burn off all the sticky dust,
Will fire off the shadows and the musk,
That has sheltered us in a winter's
Awful storm,
And readied us for sunlight
In our sleek and oiled form.

VIBRATIONS

All that is in the isles of space,
Works in a strange, vibrant pace,
To factor in the shells of atoms new,
The waves of time tell matter
What to do.
All is an oscillation in a field,
A field whose mellow motions
Soon will yield,
All the subtle joys of this creation,
And make of men a sonic jubilation.

LOVE IS, LOVE WAS

Love is and love was
Always built of sorrow and regret,
Fed by honor and white lies,
Preparing our hearts
For the breaking it must bear,
Love sweeps into our life
Like a giant broom,
And then is made to sweep,
Too late for clinging crumbs,
Buried far too deep,
Love is the sweet light that enters in,
To our hearts that break and never mend,
And maybe our heart is stronger for the break,
That scars itself to wholeness in the wake,
But I have never to complain,
For in the fields of rapture I have lain,
Which is more than all the dead do know,
And all the unloved can ever show,
For all their weary time under the rain,
Though love is, love was, always cased in pain.

IS IT HATE THAT FUELS ALL POWER?

Is it hate that fuels the powers of the world?
Is it anger for what is lost that brings us down?
What of love and peace and noble things,
What is it that moves all men to sink
From the goodness in their souls?

Who has not seen that earth is full and ripe?
So why beat its futile proddings with a stripe,
When all the air requires is our breath,
That lingers in our being until death.

UNTIL THE NIGHT

Until the night comes,
I am free,
Expanding into moments,
In eternity.

Until the night comes,
I will think,
And raise the truth from
Slumber deep,
And discover how to prosper
And to weep.

Until the night comes,
I am free,
And chase a golden rainbow
As I wait,
To enter into night's everlasting,
And unguarded, gilded gate.

0-595-24310-X